OBJECT TRACKING METHODS WITH OPENCV AND TKINTER

VIVIAN SIAHAAN
RISMON HASIHOLAN SIANIPAR

Copyright © 2024 BALIGE Publishing

All rights reserved. No part of this book may be reproduced, stored in a retrieval system, or transmitted in any form or by any means, without the prior written permission of the publisher, except in the case of brief quotations embedded in critical articles or reviews. Every effort has been made in the preparation of this book to ensure the accuracy of the information presented. However, the information contained in this book is sold without warranty, either express or implied. Neither the authors, nor BALIGE Publishing or its dealers and distributors, will be held liable for any damages caused or alleged to have been caused directly or indirectly by this book. BALIGE Publishing has endeavored to provide trademark information about all of the companies and products mentioned in this book by the appropriate use of capitals. However, BALIGE Publishing cannot guarantee the accuracy of this information.

Published: APRIL 2024
Production reference: 0500424
Published by BALIGE Publishing Ltd.
BALIGE, North Sumatera

ABOUT THE AUTHOR

Vivian Siahaan is a highly motivated individual with a passion for continuous learning and exploring new areas. Born and raised in Hinalang Bagasan, Balige, situated on the picturesque banks of Lake Toba, she completed her high school education at SMAN 1 Balige. Vivian's journey into the world of programming began with a deep dive into various languages such as Java, Android, JavaScript, CSS, C++, Python, R, Visual Basic, Visual C#, MATLAB, Mathematica, PHP, JSP, MySQL, SQL Server, Oracle, Access, and more. Starting from scratch, Vivian diligently studied programming, focusing on mastering the fundamental syntax and logic. She honed her skills by creating practical GUI applications, gradually building her expertise. One particular area of interest for Vivian is animation and game development, where she aspires to make significant contributions. Alongside her programming and mathematical pursuits, she also finds joy in indulging in novels, nurturing her love for literature. Vivian Siahaan's passion for programming and her extensive knowledge are reflected in the numerous ebooks she has authored. Her works, published by Sparta Publisher, cover a wide range of topics, including "Data Structure with Java," "Java Programming: Cookbook," "C++ Programming: Cookbook," "C Programming For High Schools/Vocational Schools and Students," "Java Programming for SMA/SMK," "Java Tutorial: GUI, Graphics and Animation," "Visual Basic Programming: From A to Z," "Java Programming for Animation and Games," "C# Programming for SMA/SMK and Students," "MATLAB For Students and Researchers," "Graphics in JavaScript: Quick Learning Series," "JavaScript Image Processing Methods: From A to Z," "Java GUI Case Study: AWT & Swing," "Basic CSS and JavaScript," "PHP/MySQL Programming: Cookbook," "Visual Basic: Cookbook," "C++ Programming for High Schools/Vocational Schools and Students," "Concepts and Practices of C++," "PHP/MySQL For Students," "C# Programming: From A to Z," "Visual Basic for SMA/SMK and Students," and "C# .NET and SQL Server for High School/Vocational School and Students." Furthermore, at the ANDI Yogyakarta publisher, Vivian Siahaan has contributed to several notable books, including "Python Programming Theory and Practice," "Python GUI Programming," "Python GUI and Database," "Build From Zero School Database Management System In Python/MySQL," "Database Management System in Python/MySQL," "Python/MySQL For Management Systems of Criminal Track Record Database," "Java/MySQL For Management Systems of Criminal Track Records Database," "Database and Cryptography Using Java/MySQL," and "Build From Zero School Database Management System With Java/MySQL." Vivian's diverse range of expertise in programming languages, combined with her passion for exploring new horizons, makes her a dynamic and versatile individual in the field of technology. Her dedication to learning, coupled with her strong analytical and problem-solving skills, positions her as a valuable asset in any programming endeavor. Vivian Siahaan's contributions to the world of programming and literature continue to inspire and empower aspiring programmers and readers alike.

Rismon Hasiholan Sianipar, born in Pematang Siantar in 1994, is a distinguished researcher and expert in the field of electrical engineering. After completing his education at SMAN 3 Pematang Siantar, Rismon ventured to the city of Jogjakarta to pursue his academic journey. He obtained his Bachelor of Engineering (S.T) and Master of Engineering (M.T) degrees in Electrical Engineering from Gadjah Mada University in 1998 and 2001, respectively, under the guidance of esteemed professors, Dr. Adhi Soesanto and Dr. Thomas Sri Widodo. During his studies, Rismon focused on researching non-stationary signals and their energy analysis using time-frequency maps. He explored the dynamic nature of signal energy distribution on time-frequency maps and developed innovative techniques using discrete wavelet transformations to design non-linear filters for data pattern analysis. His research showcased the application of these techniques in various fields. In recognition of his academic prowess, Rismon was awarded the prestigious Monbukagakusho scholarship by the Japanese Government in 2003. He went on to pursue his Master of Engineering (M.Eng) and Doctor of Engineering (Dr.Eng) degrees at Yamaguchi University, supervised by Prof. Dr. Hidetoshi Miike. Rismon's master's and doctoral theses revolved around combining the SR-FHN (Stochastic Resonance Fitzhugh-Nagumo) filter strength with the cryptosystem ECC (elliptic curve cryptography) 4096-bit. This innovative approach effectively suppressed noise in digital images and videos while ensuring their authenticity. Rismon's research findings have been published in renowned international scientific journals, and his patents have been officially registered in Japan. Notably, one of his patents, with registration number 2008-009549, gained recognition. He actively collaborates with several universities and research institutions in Japan, specializing in cryptography, cryptanalysis, and digital forensics, particularly in the areas of audio, image, and video analysis. With a passion for knowledge sharing, Rismon has authored numerous national and international scientific articles and authored several national books. He has also actively participated in workshops related to cryptography, cryptanalysis, digital watermarking, and digital forensics. During these workshops, Rismon has assisted Prof. Hidetoshi Miike in developing applications related to digital image and video processing, steganography, cryptography, watermarking, and more, which serve as valuable training materials. Rismon's field of interest encompasses multimedia security, signal processing, digital image and video analysis, cryptography, digital communication, digital forensics, and data compression. He continues to advance his research by developing applications using programming languages such as Python, MATLAB, C++, C, VB.NET, C#.NET, R, and Java. These applications serve both research and commercial purposes, further contributing to the advancement of signal and image analysis. Rismon Hasiholan Sianipar is a dedicated researcher and expert in the field of electrical engineering, particularly in the areas of signal processing, cryptography, and digital forensics. His academic achievements, patented inventions, and extensive publications demonstrate his commitment to advancing knowledge in these fields. Rismon's contributions to academia and his collaborations with prestigious institutions in Japan have solidified his position as a respected figure in the scientific community. Through his ongoing research and development of innovative applications, Rismon continues to make significant contributions to the field of electrical engineering.

ABOUT THE BOOK

The first project, BoostingTracker.py, is a Python application that leverages the Tkinter library for creating a graphical user interface (GUI) to track objects in video sequences. By utilizing OpenCV for the underlying video processing and object tracking mechanics, alongside imageio for handling video files, PIL for image displays, and matplotlib for visualization tasks, the script facilitates robust tracking capabilities. At the heart of the application is the BoostingTracker class, which orchestrates the GUI setup, video loading, and management of tracking states like playing, pausing, or stopping the video, along with enabling frame-by-frame navigation and zoom functionalities.

Upon launching, the application allows users to load a video through a dialog interface, select an object to track by drawing a bounding box, and then observe the tracker in action as it follows the object across frames. Users can interact with the video playback through intuitive controls for adjusting the zoom level and applying various image filters such as Gaussian blur or wavelet transforms to enhance video clarity and tracking accuracy. Additional features include the display of object center coordinates in real-time and the capability to analyze color histograms of the tracked areas, providing insights into color distribution and intensity for more detailed image analysis. The BoostingTracker.py combines these features into a comprehensive package that supports extensive customization and robust error handling, making it a valuable tool for applications ranging from surveillance to multimedia content analysis.

The second project, MedianFlowTracker, utilizes the Python Tkinter GUI library to provide a robust platform for video-based object tracking using the MedianFlow algorithm, renowned for its effectiveness in tracking small and slow-moving objects. The application facilitates user interaction through a feature-rich interface where users can load videos, select objects within frames via mouse inputs, and use playback controls such as play, pause, and stop. Users can also navigate through video frames and utilize a zoom feature for detailed inspections of specific areas, enhancing the usability and accessibility of video analysis.

Beyond basic tracking, the MedianFlowTracker offers advanced customization options allowing adjustments to tracking parameters like window size and the number of grid points, catering to diverse tracking needs across different video types. The application also includes a variety of image processing filters such as Gaussian blur, median filtering, and more sophisticated methods like anisotropic diffusion and wavelet transforms, which users can apply to video frames to either improve tracking outcomes or explore image processing techniques.

These features, combined with the potential for easy integration of new algorithms and enhancements due to its modular design, make the MedianFlowTracker a valuable tool for educational, research, and practical applications in digital image processing and video analysis.

The third project, MILTracker, leverages Python's Tkinter GUI library to provide a sophisticated tool for tracking objects in video sequences using the Multiple Instance Learning (MIL) tracking algorithm. This application excels in environments where the training instances might be ambiguously labeled, treating groups of pixels as "bags" to effectively handle occlusions and visual complexities in videos. Users can dynamically interact with the video, initializing tracking by selecting objects with a bounding box and adjusting tracking parameters in real-time to suit various scenarios.

The application interface is intuitive, offering functionalities like video playback control, zoom adjustments, frame navigation, and the application of various image processing filters to improve tracking accuracy. It supports extensive customization through an adjustable control panel that allows modification of tracking windows, grid points, and other algorithm-specific parameters. Additionally, the MILTracker logs the movement trajectory of tracked objects, providing valuable data for analysis and further refinement of the tracking process. Designed for extensibility, the architecture facilitates the integration of new tracking methods and enhancements, making it a versatile tool for applications ranging from surveillance to sports analysis.

The fourth project, MOSSETracker, is a GUI application crafted with Python's Tkinter library, utilizing the MOSSE (Minimum Output Sum of Squared Error) tracking algorithm to enhance real-time object tracking within video sequences. Aimed at users with interests in computer vision, the application combines essential video playback functionalities with powerful object tracking capabilities through the integration of OpenCV. This setup provides an accessible platform for those looking to delve into the dynamics of video processing and tracking technologies.

Structured for ease of use, the application presents a straightforward interface that includes video controls, zoom adjustments, and display of tracked object coordinates. Users can initiate tracking by selecting an object within the video through a draggable bounding box, which the MOSSE algorithm uses to maintain tracking across frames. Additionally, the application offers a suite of image processing filters like Gaussian blur and wavelet transformations to enhance tracking accuracy or demonstrate processing techniques. Overall, MOSSETracker not only facilitates effective object tracking but also serves as an educational tool, allowing users to experiment with and learn about advanced video analysis and tracking methods within a practical, user-friendly environment.

The fifth project, KCFTracker, is utilizing Kernelized Correlation Filters (KCF) for object tracking, is a comprehensive application built using Python. It incorporates several libraries such as Tkinter for GUI development, OpenCV for robust image processing, and ImageIO for video stream handling. This application offers an intuitive GUI that allows users to upload videos, manually draw bounding boxes to identify areas of interest, and adjust tracking parameters in real-time to optimize performance. Key features include the ability to apply a variety of image filters to enhance video quality and tracking accuracy under varying conditions, and advanced functionalities like real-time tracking updates and histogram analysis for in-depth examination of color distributions within the video frame. This melding of interactive elements, real-time processing capabilities, and analytical tools establishes the MILTracker as a versatile and educational platform for those delving into computer vision.

The sixth project, CSRT (Channel and Spatial Reliability Tracker), features a high-performance tracking algorithm encapsulated in a Python application that integrates OpenCV and the Tkinter graphical user interface, making it a versatile tool for precise object tracking in various applications like surveillance and autonomous vehicle navigation. The application offers a user-friendly interface that includes video playback, interactive controls for real-time parameter adjustments, and manual bounding box adjustments to initiate and guide the tracking process.

The CSRT tracker is adept at handling variations in object appearance, lighting, and occlusions due to its utilization of both channel reliability and spatial information, enhancing its effectiveness across challenging scenarios. The application not only facilitates robust tracking but also provides tools for video frame preprocessing, such as Gaussian blur and adaptive thresholding, which are essential for optimizing tracking accuracy. Additional features like zoom controls, frame navigation, and advanced analytical tools, including histogram analysis and wavelet transformations, further enrich the user experience and provide deep insights into the video content being analyzed.

CONTENT

OBJECT TRACKING WITH BOOSTING TRACKER	1
DESCRIPTION	1
IMPORTING LIBRARIES	3
CLASS AND INITIALIZATION	5
CREATING WIDGETS	8
MANAGING VIDEO PLAYBACK	12
INITIALIZING TRACKER	15
TRACKING OBJECT	17
UPDATING BOUNDING BOX RECTANGLE	20
SHOWING FRAME	22
HANDLING MOUSE EVENTS	26
NAVIGATING FRAMES	29
SETTING WINDOW TITILE	31
CLEARING LIST WIDGET	33
ANALYZING HISTOGRAM	35
CREATING POPUP WINDOW	38
DISPLAYING CROPPED IMAGE	40
DISPLAYING HISTOGRAM	42
DISPLAYING LINE HISTOGRAM	44
DISPLAYING BAR HISTOGRAM	48
GENERATING HISTOGRAM IMAGE	51
GENERATING HISTOGRAM BAR IMAGE	54
CONVERTING MATPLOTLIB INTO IMAGE	57
APPLYING FILTERS	58
DEFINING WIENER FILTER	62
DEFINING ADAPTIVE THRESHOLD FILTER	64
DEFINING HAAR FILTER	67
DEFINING DAUBECHIES FILTER	70
DEFINING ANISOTROPIC DIFFUSION	73
APPLYING TOTAL VARIATION DENOISING	74
DEFINING TOTAL VARIATION DENOISING	77
ENTRY POINT FOR APPLICATION	80
RUNNING PROGRAM	82
SOURCE CODE	85

OBJECT TRACKING WITH MEDIAN FLOW TRACKER — 100
- DESCRIPTION — 100
- CREATING WIDGETS — 102
- INIITALIZING TRACKER — 107
- TRACKING OBJECT — 111
- RUNNING PROGRAM — 114

OBJECT TRACKING WITH MIL (MULTIPLE INSTANCE LEARNING) TRACKER — 117
- DESCRIPTION — 117
- TRACKING OBJECT — 119
- RUNNING PROGRAM — 122

OBJECT TRACKING WITH MOSSE (MINIMUM OUTPUT SUM OF SQUARED ERROR) TRACKER — 126
- DESCRIPTION — 126
- TRACKING OBJECT — 127
- RUNNING PROGRAM — 130

OBJECT TRACKING WITH MOSSE KCF (KERNELIZED CORRELATION FILTERS) TRACKER — 133
- DESCRIPTION — 133
- TRACKING OBJECT — 135
- RUNNING PROGRAM — 139

OBJECT TRACKING WITH CSRT (CHANNEL AND SPATIAL RELIABILITY TRACKER) — 142
- DESCRIPTION — 142
- TRACKING OBJECT — 144
- RUNNING PROGRAM — 148
- SOURCE CODE — 151

Bibliography — 166

OBJECT TRACKING WITH BOOSTING TRACKER

DESCRIPTION

The BoostingTracker.py script is an advanced application developed using Python and the Tkinter library, designed for object tracking within videos. The script integrates multiple libraries, including OpenCV for video processing and tracking, imageio for video file handling, PIL for image display, and matplotlib for visualization. The core functionality centers around a class named BoostingTracker that handles the GUI and tracking logic.

The script begins by importing necessary libraries and initializing the BoostingTracker class with a constructor that sets up the main window, controls, and initial states such as paused, tracking, and video loading status. This class manages the user interface where users can interact with the application, including buttons for playing, pausing, stopping, and navigating through the video. It also includes functionality to open and display video files, drawing bounding boxes for object tracking, and adjusting zoom levels.

A key component of this script is the method to open a video file, which utilizes a file dialog for the user to select a video. Once a video is loaded, its frames are displayed on a canvas where users can play or pause the video, navigate frame by frame, or stop the video altogether. The GUI also allows for zooming in and out of the video frames, enhancing user interaction and visibility.

The tracker functionality is initialized when the user selects an area on the video frame, which sets the bounding box for tracking. The application uses OpenCV's legacy TrackerBoosting class, which implements a boosting tracker algorithm to track objects in video frames. Users can manually define the initial bounding box by clicking and dragging over the object of interest, which the tracker will then use to follow the object across the frames.

The GUI also includes a list box that displays the center coordinates of the tracked object, updating continuously as the video plays. This feature provides visual feedback on the tracking accuracy and the movement of the object within the video. A variety of image filters can be applied to the video frames or the selected object, including Gaussian, median, and bilateral filtering, as well as wavelet transforms and adaptive thresholding. These filters can be selected from a dropdown menu, enhancing the versatility of the application in processing different video conditions.

In addition to tracking and display functionalities, the script can analyze histograms of the selected regions within the video frames. This is done through a popup window that shows both the cropped image and its color histograms, allowing for a deeper analysis of the color distribution and intensity within the tracked object. This feature is particularly useful for applications requiring detailed image analysis and color information.

Error handling is a significant aspect of the application, ensuring that operations like video playback, frame processing, and tracking are smoothly handled even when encountering corrupted data or file read errors. The script gracefully manages such exceptions by displaying error messages and resetting states as necessary.

The application also provides a robust interface for customizing tracking parameters, such as the scale of the bounding box and the selection of different filtering options. This customization enhances the adaptability of the tracker to different objects and conditions within the video.

Overall, BoostingTracker.py is a comprehensive tool for video analysis, providing robust object tracking capabilities along with advanced image processing features. It serves as a practical application for users needing detailed analysis and visualization of video data, applicable in various fields such as surveillance, research, and multimedia.

IMPORTING LIBRARIES

```
import tkinter as tk
from tkinter import ttk
from tkinter import filedialog
from PIL import Image, ImageTk
import imageio
import cv2
import numpy as np
import matplotlib.pyplot as plt
import pywt
```

These libraries are used for different purposes, each contributing to building a comprehensive application. Here's a breakdown of each import and its role:
   1. tkinter and ttk:

- tkinter is Python's standard GUI (Graphical User Interface) toolkit. It provides various widgets and controls such as buttons, labels, text entries, and more, used for building the interface of desktop applications.
- ttk (themed tkinter) is a module that provides access to the Tk themed widget set, which enhances the visual appearance of the GUI by allowing different themes to be applied.

2. filedialog:

Part of tkinter, filedialog allows the user to interact with the file system, enabling operations like opening and saving files. This is particularly useful for applications that need to load or save media files like images or videos.

3. PIL (Pillow) and ImageTk:
   - PIL (Python Imaging Library), now known as Pillow, is a library for opening, manipulating, and saving many different image file formats. It's extensively used in applications that need image processing capabilities.
   - ImageTk is a module in Pillow that allows images processed by Pillow to be displayed in tkinter applications. This is essential for rendering images on the GUI.

4. imageio:

imageio is a Python library that provides an easy interface to read and write a wide range of image data, including animated images, video streams, and volumetric data. This is useful for applications dealing with video processing.

5. cv2:

cv2 is the OpenCV (Open Source Computer Vision Library) module for Python, which is used for real-time computer vision. It allows for processing and analysis of images and videos, including operations like object detection, face recognition, and motion tracking.

6. numpy:

numpy is a fundamental package for scientific computing with Python. It provides support for large, multi-dimensional arrays and matrices, along with a large collection of high-level mathematical functions to operate on these arrays. It's often used in image and video processing for data manipulation and operations.

7. matplotlib.pyplot:

matplotlib is a plotting library for the Python programming language and its numerical mathematics extension numpy. pyplot is a module in matplotlib that provides a MATLAB-like interface for making plots, graphs, and charts. It can be used to visualize data and results from image and video analysis.

8. pywt:

pywt is the PyWavelets library, which provides a complete approach to wavelet analysis, useful in image processing for tasks like denoising or feature extraction. Wavelets are particularly good at representing data with sharp discontinuities and can be a powerful tool for image compression and noise reduction.

Each of these libraries plays a crucial role in building applications that require interactive, real-time processing and analysis of images and videos with a user-friendly graphical interface.

CLASS AND INITIALIZATION

```
class BoostingTracker:
    def __init__(self, master):
        self.master = master
        self.master.title("Object Tracking with Boosting Tracker")
        self.file_name = ""
        self.set_window_title()  # Set window title initially

        self.frame_number_label = tk.Label(master, text="Frame: 0")
        self.frame_number_label.pack()

        self.video = None
```

```
            self.video_path = None
            self.paused = False
            self.zoom_scale = tk.IntVar(value=1)
            self.frame_index = 0
            self.bbox = None
            self.bbox2 = None
            self.tracking_started = False  # Initialize tracking_started to False
            self.prev_frame_gray = None
            self.tracker = None
            self.initial_w = None
            self.initial_h = None
            self.bbox_rect = None  # Initialize bbox_rect attribute to None
            self.frame_processing = False  # Initialize frame_processing attribute to
False

            # Available filters
            self.filters = ["None", "Gaussian", "Mean", "Median", "Bilateral Filtering",
                        "Non-local Means Denoising", "Anisotropic Diffusion",
                        "Total Variation Denoising", "Wiener Filter",
                        "Adaptive Thresholding", "Haar Wavelet Transform",
                        "Daubechies Wavelet Transform"]

            self.create_widgets()
```

The BoostingTracker class initializes a Tkinter application dedicated to object tracking in video streams. Here's a detailed breakdown of its functionality, highlighting each component of the class constructor and the purposes they serve:

1. Initialization and Setup

    - Master Window Configuration: The constructor accepts a master parameter, typically an instance of tk.Tk(). This serves as the main window for the application. The title of the window is set to "Object Tracking with Boosting Tracker".

    - File Name: A placeholder self.file_name is initialized to keep track of the current video file name, which is empty initially.

    - Frame Number Label: A Tkinter Label widget is created to display the current frame number in the video. This is packed into the main window using pack() which is a geometry manager that organizes widgets in blocks before placing them in the parent widget.

2. Video Processing Attributes
    - Video Handling: self.video and self.video_path are initialized to None, prepared to store the video reader object and the path to the current video file, respectively.
    - Playback Control: The self.paused boolean attribute is used to control the play/pause state of the video.
    - Zoom Feature: self.zoom_scale is an integer variable (using tk.IntVar) to handle the zoom level of the video display.
    - Frame Index and Bounding Box: self.frame_index keeps track of the current frame being displayed. self.bbox and self.bbox2 are initialized to None and used for storing bounding box coordinates during object tracking.
    - Tracking Flags: self.tracking_started, self.prev_frame_gray, and self.tracker are used to manage the state and functionality of the object tracking. self.tracking_started checks if tracking has begun, while self.tracker would typically be an OpenCV tracking object.
    - Initial Dimensions and Rectangle: self.initial_w and self.initial_h store the initial dimensions of the bounding box, and self.bbox_rect keeps a reference to the bounding box rectangle drawn on the Tkinter canvas.
    - Frame Processing: self.frame_processing is a flag to manage frame updates and avoid conflicts or overloads in frame processing.

3. Filters

Image Filters: A list of self.filters contains various image processing options that can be applied to the video frames. These include blurring, noise reduction, edge preserving filters, and wavelet transforms. Each filter represents a method to alter the visual characteristics of frames for enhanced tracking or analysis.

4. Widget Creation

    Create Widgets: The create_widgets() method (not shown in your snippet) is likely responsible for creating the GUI components such as buttons, sliders, and other interactive elements. It's critical for setting up the user interface, enabling user interactions like starting or stopping video playback, adjusting zoom, selecting filters, and manipulating the video display.

This class sets up a robust foundation for a video tracking application. The GUI built through Tkinter allows for real-time interaction with video streams, and the integration with OpenCV enables sophisticated image processing and object tracking capabilities. This setup is ideal for applications in areas like surveillance, sports analysis, or any field requiring monitoring of moving objects in video data.

CREATING WIDGETS

```python
def create_widgets(self):
    # Panel for video display
    video_panel = tk.Frame(self.master)
    video_panel.pack(padx=10, pady=10)

    # Canvas to display the original video
    canvas_width = 800
    canvas_height = 500
    self.canvas = tk.Canvas(video_panel, width=canvas_width, height=canvas_height)
    self.canvas.pack(side="left", fill="both", expand=True)
    self.canvas.bind("<MouseWheel>", self.on_mousewheel)
    self.canvas.bind("<ButtonPress-1>", self.on_press)
    self.canvas.bind("<B1-Motion>", self.on_drag)
    self.canvas.bind("<ButtonRelease-1>", self.on_release)  # Bind ButtonRelease event

    # List box to display center coordinates
    self.center_listbox = tk.Listbox(video_panel, width=30, height=20, font=("Helvetica", 14))
    self.center_listbox.pack(side="right", fill="y")
```

```python
        # Scrollbar for the listbox
        scrollbar = tk.Scrollbar(video_panel, orient="vertical")
        scrollbar.pack(side="left", fill="y")
        scrollbar.config(command=self.center_listbox.yview)

        # Attach scrollbar to listbox
        self.center_listbox.config(yscrollcommand=scrollbar.set)

        # Panel for control buttons
        control_panel = tk.Frame(self.master)
        control_panel.pack(padx=10, pady=(0, 10), fill="x")

        # Button to open a video file
        self.open_button = tk.Button(control_panel, text="Open Video", command=self.open_video)
        self.open_button.grid(row=0, column=0, padx=10, pady=5)

        # Combobox for selecting zoom scale
        self.zoom_combobox = ttk.Combobox(control_panel, textvariable=self.zoom_scale, values=list(range(1, 11)))
        self.zoom_combobox.grid(row=0, column=1, padx=10, pady=5)
        self.zoom_combobox.bind("<<ComboboxSelected>>", self.update_zoom)

        # Button to play/pause the video
        self.play_button = tk.Button(control_panel, text="Play/Pause", command=self.toggle_play_pause)
        self.play_button.grid(row=0, column=2, padx=10, pady=5)

        # Button to stop the video
        self.stop_button = tk.Button(control_panel, text="Stop", command=self.stop_video)
        self.stop_button.grid(row=0, column=3, padx=10, pady=5)

        # Button to navigate to the previous frame
        self.prev_frame_button = tk.Button(control_panel, text="Previous Frame", command=self.prev_frame)
        self.prev_frame_button.grid(row=0, column=4, padx=10, pady=5)

        # Button to navigate to the next frame
        self.next_frame_button = tk.Button(control_panel, text="Next Frame", command=self.next_frame)
        self.next_frame_button.grid(row=0, column=5, padx=10, pady=5)

        # Button to clear the listbox
        self.clear_button = tk.Button(control_panel, text="Clear Listbox", command=self.clear_listbox)
        self.clear_button.grid(row=0, column=6, padx=10, pady=5)
```

```
# Label and entry for specifying scale
self.scale_label = tk.Label(control_panel, text="Scale:")
self.scale_label.grid(row=0, column=7, padx=10, pady=5, sticky="e")
self.scale_default = tk.StringVar(value="1")
self.scale_entry = ttk.Entry(control_panel, textvariable=self.scale_default)
self.scale_entry.grid(row=0, column=8, padx=10, pady=5, sticky="w")
self.scale_entry.bind("<Return>", lambda event: self.toggle_play_pause())

# Combobox for selecting filters
self.filter_combobox = ttk.Combobox(control_panel, values=self.filters)
self.filter_combobox.grid(row=0, column=9, padx=10, pady=5)
self.filter_combobox.current(0)  # Set default value
```

The create_widgets() method in your BoostingTracker class defines and organizes the various GUI components that make up the user interface for your object tracking application. Here's a detailed look at each component and how they contribute to the application's functionality:

Video Display Panel
- Video Panel: This is a tk.Frame that acts as a container for the video display and tracking interface. It is packed with padding to separate it from other UI elements, providing clear visual sections in the GUI.
- Canvas: A tk.Canvas is created to actually display video frames. It's set to a fixed width and height but can expand and fill space as needed. The canvas is bound to mouse events (wheel, press, drag, release) to handle zooming and object tracking via user interactions like drawing bounding boxes.

List Box for Tracking Data
- List Box: Positioned on the right side of the video panel, this widget displays the center coordinates of the tracked object. It's useful for monitoring tracking accuracy and provides a direct output of the results.
- Scrollbar: Enhances the list box by adding vertical scrolling capability, which is necessary for usability when many entries are added.

Control Panel for Video Interaction
- Control Buttons: This set of buttons includes functionalities like opening a video file, toggling playback, stopping the video, and navigating through frames. These controls are essential for user interaction with the video stream, allowing for dynamic and controlled viewing.
- Zoom Combobox: A dropdown menu that lets users select the zoom level of the video display, enhancing the viewability of details within video frames. It's connected to an event that updates the zoom level in the application.
- Scale Entry: Allows users to enter a scaling factor manually and apply it by pressing the "Enter" key. This can adjust the size of the tracking bounding box or other scalable parameters in the application.
- Clear Button: Provides functionality to clear the entries in the list box, which is useful for resetting the tracking data display without restarting the application.

Filtering Options
- Filter Combobox: Allows users to select from a variety of predefined image filters to apply to the video or tracked object. This is important for experimenting with different image processing techniques to enhance tracking performance or visual clarity.
- Layout and Interaction
- Grid Layout: The controls are arranged using the grid layout manager, which allows precise placement of widgets in a tabular form. This layout choice facilitates an organized and easily understandable user interface.
- Event Bindings: Widgets like the combobox for zoom and the scale entry field have event bindings that trigger specific functions, tying the UI controls to backend functionalities. For example, changing the zoom level in the combobox automatically triggers an update in the video display.

Overall, this method efficiently sets up a comprehensive GUI for a video tracking application. It provides essential tools for interaction, such as playback control, zoom adjustments, and filter application, all crucial for a user-friendly experience in video analysis and object tracking tasks. The arrangement ensures that the interface is not only functional but also intuitive, allowing users to easily manipulate video data and observe the effects of different processing techniques in real-time.

MANAGING VIDEO PLAYBACK

```python
def open_video(self):
    self.video_path = filedialog.askopenfilename(filetypes=[("Video files",
"*.mp4;*.avi;*.mkv;*.wmv")])
    if self.video_path:
        self.video = imageio.get_reader(self.video_path)
        self.file_name = self.video_path.split('/')[-1]
        self.set_window_title()
        self.play_video()

def play_video(self):
    if self.video:
        self.paused = False
        self.tracking_started = True
        self.show_frame()

def stop_video(self):
    self.paused = True
    self.frame_index = 0
    self.bbox = None
    self.tracker = None  # Reset tracker
    self.initial_w = None  # Reset width
    self.initial_h = None  # Reset height
    self.show_frame()

def toggle_play_pause(self):
    self.paused = not self.paused
    if not self.paused:
        if self.bbox is not None:
            self.tracking_started = True
        self.play_video()
```

The methods —open_video(), play_video(), stop_video(), and toggle_play_pause()— provide essential controls for managing video playback in the BoostingTracker application. Here's an analysis of each method and how they contribute to the application's functionality:

open_video() Method

- File Dialog: Opens a file dialog window allowing the user to select a video file from their file system. The filetypes parameter restricts the selection to common video formats such as MP4, AVI, MKV, and WMV, ensuring compatibility.
- Video Reader: Utilizes the imageio library to create a video reader object (self.video) from the selected file path (self.video_path). This reader is used to fetch video frames for processing and display.
- File Name Extraction: Splits the selected file path to extract the file name, which is used to update the window title for better user orientation.
- Playback Initiation: Calls the play_video() method to start video playback immediately after a file is loaded.

play_video() Method

- Playback Start: Checks if a video is loaded (self.video is not None). If true, it resets the self.paused flag to False and sets self.tracking_started to True, indicating that video playback and tracking can proceed.
- Frame Display: Calls show_frame to display the first frame (or the next frame in the sequence, depending on the state of self.frame_index).

stop_video() Method

- Pause and Reset: Sets self.paused to True, indicating that the video should stop playing. It also resets the self.frame_index to 0, effectively rewinding the video to the beginning.
- Tracking Reset: Clears the current tracking bounding box (self.bbox), tracker object (self.tracker), and the dimensions associated with the bounding box (self.initial_w and self.initial_h).
- Update Display: Calls show_frame() to update the canvas, likely clearing any remaining images or drawings related to the video frames.

toggle_play_pause() Method

- Play/Pause Toggle: Flips the state of the self.paused flag. If the video is currently paused, it resumes playback; if it is playing, it pauses.
- Conditional Playback: If the video is set to play (i.e., self.paused is False after the toggle), it checks if a bounding box (self.bbox) exists, implying there's an object being tracked. If so, it sets self.tracking_started to True and then calls play_video to continue playing from the current frame.

These methods collectively manage the video playback controls, allowing users to open new videos, start/stop playback, and toggle between play and pause states seamlessly. They handle the integration of video loading, playback, and tracking state management in a user-friendly manner, making the application robust for tasks such as object tracking and video analysis.

INITIALIZING TRACKER

```python
def initialize_tracker(self, frame, bbox, params=None):
    """Initialize the tracker with possible user-defined parameters."""
    if params:
        # Here you could adjust bbox based on params, if params affect size, etc.
        scale = int(self.scale_entry.get())  # Get threshold from entry
        bbox = (
            bbox[0], bbox[1],
            int(bbox[2] * scale), int(bbox[3] * scale)
        )

    # Initialize the tracker
    self.tracker = cv2.legacy.TrackerBoosting_create()
    self.tracker.init(frame, tuple(map(int, bbox)))
    self.initial_w, self.initial_h = bbox[2], bbox[3]
```

The initialize_tracker() method is a crucial function within BoostingTracker application, designed to set up and configure the object tracking functionality using OpenCV's Boosting Tracker. Here's a step-by-step breakdown of how this method works:

Purpose of the Method

This method initializes the tracking system with user-defined or pre-defined parameters. It configures the tracker to follow an object identified by a bounding box (bbox) on a video frame.

Method Parameters

- frame: The current frame from the video where the tracker should start tracking. This is typically the frame where the object has been identified.
- bbox: A tuple of the form (x, y, width, height) that specifies the rectangle defining the boundaries of the object to track.
- params: Optional parameters that could modify the behavior or settings of the tracker. These include adjustments to scale, sensitivity, or other tracking-related settings.

Method Operations
1. Parameter Handling:
    - If params are provided, the method includes functionality to adjust the bounding box based on these parameters. This example shows how to handle a scale change by reading a scaling factor from a GUI entry widget (self.scale_entry).
    - The bounding box dimensions (width and height) are scaled according to the user-provided scale factor, allowing the tracker to adapt to user preferences for object size in tracking.
2. Tracker Initialization:
    - The method initializes an instance of OpenCV's Boosting Tracker using cv2.legacy.TrackerBoosting_create(). This tracker is part of OpenCV's legacy support for various tracking algorithms and is known for its ability to handle occlusion and variability in object appearance, though it might not be the fastest or most accurate compared to newer algorithms like KCF or CSRT.
    - The tracker is then initialized with the current frame and the adjusted bounding box using tracker.init(frame, tuple(map(int, bbox))). This step sets the tracker to start following the object defined by the bbox.
3. Tracking Metrics Setup:

    After initializing the tracker, the method stores the dimensions of the bounding box (width and height) in self.initial_w and self.initial_h. These values are used to maintain a consistent size of the tracking box as the video plays, which is crucial for visual consistency and accuracy in tracking.

Summary

The initialize_tracker() method efficiently sets up the object tracking system by interfacing OpenCV's tracking capabilities with the GUI elements of your application. It allows for dynamic adjustments to the tracking parameters via the GUI, enhancing user interaction and flexibility in tracking various objects under different conditions. This method is foundational for applications involving video surveillance, sports analytics, or any scenario where following the movement of objects in video streams is necessary.

TRACKING OBJECT

```python
def track_object(self, frame, bbox, user_params=None):
    """Track object using Boosting Tracker with optional user parameters."""
    if bbox:
        if self.tracker is None:
            self.initialize_tracker(frame, bbox, user_params)

        # Update the tracker and get the new bounding box
        success, bbox = self.tracker.update(frame)
        if success:
            x1, y1, w, h = map(int, bbox)
            # Use stored initial dimensions
            w, h = self.initial_w, self.initial_h
            x2, y2 = x1 + w, y1 + h

            # Calculate and display the center of the bounding box
            center_x = (x1 + x2) // 2
            center_y = (y1 + y2) // 2
            self.center_listbox.insert(tk.END, f"(center_x = {center_x}, center_y = {center_y})")

            return x1, y1, x2, y2
    return None
```

The track_object() method within BoostingTracker class plays a critical role in maintaining the continuity of object tracking across video frames. This method integrates closely with the initialized tracker to dynamically update the tracking box as the video plays. Here's a detailed explanation of how this method functions:

Functionality Overview

The method aims to continue tracking an object specified by a bounding box (bbox) in successive video frames. It leverages OpenCV's Boosting Tracker to handle the actual tracking logic, providing robust tracking even when the object undergoes variations in appearance or movement.

Parameters

- frame: The current video frame in which the object is to be tracked.
- bbox: A tuple (x, y, width, height) representing the initial or previously known position and dimensions of the object.
- user_params: Optional parameters that might influence how the tracking is performed, such as scaling or other adjustments.

Step-by-Step Process

1. Initialization Check:
   - The method first checks if a bounding box is provided. If there's no bounding box, the function returns None, indicating that tracking cannot proceed without an initial position.
   - If the tracker hasn't been initialized yet (self.tracker is None), it calls initialize_tracker with the current frame, the bounding box, and any user parameters. This step sets up the tracker to start following the object defined by bbox.
2. Tracker Update:
   - The method updates the tracker with the current frame using self.tracker.update(frame). This function returns a tuple (success, bbox), where success is a boolean indicating whether the tracking was successful, and bbox is the updated bounding box coordinates.

- If tracking is successful (success is True), the method extracts the updated bounding box coordinates (x1, y1, w, h) and adjusts them to use the initial dimensions (self.initial_w, self.initial_h). This adjustment ensures that the size of the tracking box remains consistent across frames, which is particularly important for visual consistency and accurate tracking.

3. Coordinate Calculation and Display:
   - Computes the center of the bounding box by calculating the midpoints between the coordinates (x1, x2) and (y1, y2). This is useful for applications that need to monitor the precise location of the tracked object within the frame.
   - Inserts the center coordinates into a Tkinter Listbox (self.center_listbox) which displays these values, providing a visual log of the object's position over time.

4. Return Values:
   - If tracking succeeds, returns the coordinates of the corners of the bounding box (x1, y1, x2, y2). This data can be used to draw the bounding box on the video display or for further processing.
   - If the bounding box is not provided or tracking fails, returns None, signaling that tracking did not proceed or was not successful.

Summary

The track_object() method is essential for continuous object tracking in video streams, enabling applications like surveillance, activity monitoring, or any context where following the movement of objects is crucial. It effectively integrates the GUI components of the application with the backend processing power of OpenCV's tracking algorithms, providing real-time tracking capabilities with visual feedback through the Tkinter interface. This method not only maintains the tracking state but also provides valuable tracking data to the user in an accessible manner.

UPDATING BOUNDING BOX RECTANGLE

```
def update_bbox_rectangle(self, bbox):
    if bbox is not None:
        x1, y1, x2, y2 = map(int, bbox)
        if self.bbox_rect is not None:
            self.canvas.coords(self.bbox_rect, x1, y1, x2, y2)
            self.canvas.tag_raise(self.bbox_rect)  # Raise the bounding box to the front
        else:
            self.bbox_rect = self.canvas.create_rectangle(x1, y1, x2, y2, outline='#fc3d3d', width=8, tags="bbox")
```

The update_bbox_rectangle() method in BoostingTracker class is designed to visually update or create a bounding box on the canvas, which represents the tracked object in the video. This method is a crucial part of the user interface because it provides real-time visual feedback about the location and movement of the object being tracked. Here's an analysis of how this method functions and its importance:

Functionality Overview

This method updates the canvas with a rectangle that outlines the tracked object, reflecting its current position in the video frame. It either modifies the coordinates of an existing rectangle or creates a new one if none exists.

Parameters

bbox: A tuple (x1, y1, x2, y2) that represents the coordinates of the rectangle bounding the object. These coordinates define the top-left (x1, y1) and bottom-right (x2, y2) corners of the rectangle.

Detailed Operation
1. Bounding Box Validation:

    The method first checks if bbox is not None, which ensures that there is valid data to work with. If bbox is None, the method does nothing, effectively skipping any updates when tracking data is unavailable or invalid.

2. Coordinate Preparation:

    Uses map(int, bbox) to ensure that all bounding box coordinates are integers, which are required for accurately drawing the rectangle on the canvas.

3. Rectangle Update or Creation:

    - Existing Rectangle: If a rectangle (self.bbox_rect) already exists on the canvas, the method updates its coordinates using self.canvas.coords(self.bbox_rect, x1, y1, x2, y2). This adjusts the rectangle to the new location of the tracked object without creating additional objects on the canvas.
    - Raising Rectangle: After updating the coordinates, it calls self.canvas.tag_raise(self.bbox_rect) to ensure the rectangle remains visually on top of other canvas elements, making it clearly visible against the video background.
    - New Rectangle Creation: If no rectangle currently exists (self.bbox_rect is None), the method creates a new rectangle on the canvas using self.canvas.create_rectangle(x1, y1, x2, y2, outline='#fc3d3d', width=8, tags="bbox"). This is done the first time an object is tracked or if the previous rectangle was removed for some reason. The rectangle is styled with a specific outline color and line width to make it distinct and visible.

Importance of Visual Feedback
- Real-Time Tracking Visualization: The bounding box provides immediate visual feedback on the effectiveness and accuracy of the tracking algorithm. Users can

see exactly where the system believes the object is, which is critical for applications like surveillance, sports analysis, or any interactive media analysis.
- User Interface Interaction: By updating the bounding box directly on the video display, the method bridges the gap between the backend tracking logic and the frontend user interaction. This makes the application intuitive and user-friendly, as changes in the object's position are instantly reflected on the screen.

Summary

The update_bbox_rectangle() method is an essential component of the BoostingTracker application, enabling dynamic visual tracking within the GUI. It ensures that users can visually monitor the tracked object, enhancing user experience and providing essential data for further analysis or interaction. This method is a key part of maintaining an interactive and responsive tracking system.

SHOWING FRAME

```
def show_frame(self):
    if self.video:
        if not self.paused:
            if 0 <= self.frame_index < len(self.video):
                if not self.frame_processing:  # Check if the frame is already being processed
                    try:
                        self.frame_processing = True  # Set frame_processing flag to True to indicate frame processing

                        frame = self.video.get_data(self.frame_index)
                        frame = cv2.cvtColor(frame, cv2.COLOR_RGB2BGR)

                        if self.bbox is not None:
                            if not self.tracking_started:
                                self.tracking_started = True

                            self.bbox = self.track_object(frame, self.bbox)
```

```
                        if self.bbox:
                            frame = cv2.cvtColor(frame, cv2.COLOR_BGR2RGB)
                            frame = Image.fromarray(frame)
                            frame = frame.resize((frame.width *
self.zoom_scale.get(), frame.height * self.zoom_scale.get()))
                            photo = ImageTk.PhotoImage(frame)
                            self.photo = photo
                            self.canvas.delete("video")
                            self.canvas.create_image(0, 0, anchor="nw",
image=photo, tags="video")

                            self.update_bbox_rectangle(self.bbox)

                        else:
                            frame = cv2.cvtColor(frame, cv2.COLOR_BGR2RGB)
                            frame = Image.fromarray(frame)
                            frame = frame.resize((frame.width *
self.zoom_scale.get(), frame.height * self.zoom_scale.get()))
                            photo = ImageTk.PhotoImage(frame)
                            self.photo = photo
                            self.canvas.delete("video")
                            self.canvas.create_image(0, 0, anchor="nw",
image=photo, tags="video")

                        self.frame_number_label.config(text=f"Frame:
{self.frame_index} / {self.video.count_frames()}", font=("Helvetica", 18))

                        self.frame_index += 1

                except Exception as e:
                    print("Error: ", e)
                finally:
                    self.frame_processing = False  # Reset frame_processing
flag to False after processing the frame
```

The show_frame() method controls the display of each frame in the video, processes the tracking of objects within those frames, and updates the GUI accordingly. It ensures that the video is played only when it is not paused and manages frame indexing to loop through the video data.

Detailed Breakdown

1. Video Existence Check:

The method first checks if the self.video object exists, ensuring there is a loaded video to display.

2. Pause Check:

If the video is paused (self.paused is True), the method does nothing and prevents further processing, effectively freezing the frame display.

3. Frame Index Validity:

The method checks if the current frame index (self.frame_index) is within the valid range of the video's frames. This prevents accessing frames outside the available range, which would lead to errors.

4. Frame Processing Flag:

It checks the self.frame_processing flag to ensure that no two frames are processed simultaneously, which could happen due to the asynchronous nature of GUI and video processing. This flag prevents race conditions and potential crashes or erratic behavior.

5. Frame Retrieval and Conversion:

Retrieves the current frame using self.video.get_data(self.frame_index) and converts it from RGB to BGR format suitable for processing with OpenCV using cv2.cvtColor(frame, cv2.COLOR_RGB2BGR).

6. Object Tracking:
   - If a bounding box (self.bbox) exists, indicating that there is an object to track, it calls self.track_object to update the position of the bounding box based on the current frame.
   - If self.tracking_started is False, it sets it to True to start the tracking process.

7. Frame Display:
   - Converts the frame back to RGB from BGR (if it was altered for tracking) to make it compatible with PIL for display.

- Resizes the image according to the self.zoom_scale, allowing users to zoom in or out.
- Converts the frame to a PhotoImage and displays it on the canvas, clearing the previous image first.

8. Bounding Box Update:

    If a bounding box is being tracked and successfully updated, it calls self.update_bbox_rectangle to redraw the bounding box on the canvas to reflect the new position of the tracked object.

9. Frame Index and Label Update:
    - Updates the self.frame_number_label to reflect the current frame number and the total frame count, providing feedback to the user about the video's progress.
    - Increments self.frame_index to proceed to the next frame on subsequent calls.

10. Exception Handling:

    Catches and prints any exceptions that occur during frame processing, which helps in diagnosing errors without crashing the application.

11. Reset Frame Processing Flag:

    Finally, resets the self.frame_processing flag to False, allowing the next frame to be processed.

Summary

The show_frame() method effectively handles multiple responsibilities: loading and displaying frames, tracking objects within those frames, and updating the GUI elements to provide a smooth and interactive user experience. By managing these tasks efficiently, the method ensures that the video tracking application can handle real-time data and user interactions without delays or errors. This method is a cornerstone of the application, tying together video playback, object tracking, and user interface management.

HANDLING MOUSE EVENTS

```python
    def on_mousewheel(self, event):
        direction = event.delta // 120
        current_value = int(self.zoom_scale.get())
        if direction == 1 and current_value < 10:
            current_value += 1
        elif direction == -1 and current_value > 1:
            current_value -= 1
        self.zoom_scale.set(current_value)
        self.update_zoom()

    def on_press(self, event):
        self.tracker = None
        self.start_x = self.canvas.canvasx(event.x)
        self.start_y = self.canvas.canvasy(event.y)
        # Clear the previous bounding box if it exists
        if self.bbox_rect:
            self.canvas.delete(self.bbox_rect)
            self.bbox_rect = None
        self.bbox = None
        self.bbox2 = None

    def on_drag(self, event):
        # Update the endpoint of the rectangle as the mouse moves
        cur_x = self.canvas.canvasx(event.x)
        cur_y = self.canvas.canvasy(event.y)

        # Define the coordinates correctly ensuring x1 < x2 and y1 < y2
        x1, y1 = min(self.start_x, cur_x), min(self.start_y, cur_y)
        x2, y2 = max(self.start_x, cur_x), max(self.start_y, cur_y)

        # Update dimensions for tracking
        self.initial_w = x2 - x1
        self.initial_h = y2 - y1
        self.bbox = (x1, y1, self.initial_w, self.initial_h)
        self.bbox2 = (self.start_x, self.start_y, cur_x, cur_y)

        # Update or create a rectangle on the canvas
        if self.bbox_rect:
            self.canvas.coords(self.bbox_rect, x1, y1, x2, y2)
        else:
            self.bbox_rect = self.canvas.create_rectangle(x1, y1, x2, y2, outline="cyan", width=6)
```

The methods on_mousewheel(), on_press(), and on_drag() handle user interactions related to zooming and selecting objects for tracking within the GUI of your BoostingTracker application. Each method is integral to providing a dynamic and interactive user experience. Here's an analysis of how these methods function and their roles in the application:

on_mousewheel() Method

1. Purpose: This method handles zooming in and out on the video display based on mouse wheel actions.
2. Functionality:
    - Direction Calculation: It determines the direction of the mouse wheel scroll. event.delta indicates the amount and direction of scroll, with positive values for scrolling up and negative for down.
    - Zoom Adjustment: Depending on the scroll direction, it increments or decrements the zoom_scale value within the limits (1 to 10). This variable controls the scale factor applied to the video display.
    - Update Call: Calls self.update_zoom(), which presumably adjusts the displayed video frame to the new zoom level, ensuring the visual scale of the video updates immediately following a change in zoom level.

on_press() Method

1. Purpose: This method initializes the process for creating a new bounding box, which can be used to select an area of the video to track.
2. Functionality:
    - Tracking Reset: Resets the current tracker instance to ensure a new tracking session can begin without interference from any previous tracking data.

- Coordinate Capture: Captures the starting point (x, y) of the mouse click on the canvas. These coordinates are relative to the canvas and serve as the anchor for drawing the new bounding box.
- Bounding Box Cleanup: If a bounding box already exists, it is removed from the canvas. This ensures that old selections are cleared when making a new selection.
- State Reset: Clears any previous bounding box data, preparing for a fresh bounding box definition.

on_drag() Method

1. Purpose: Used to dynamically update the size and position of the bounding box as the user clicks and drags the mouse across the canvas.
2. Functionality:
    - Coordinate Update: Continuously captures the current mouse position as the mouse moves, updating the endpoint of the rectangle being drawn.
    - Rectangle Definition: Calculates the corners of the rectangle using the minimum and maximum of the starting and current mouse positions, ensuring the rectangle can be drawn correctly regardless of drag direction.
    - Dimension Update for Tracking: Stores the width and height of the rectangle, which are used to initialize tracking once the mouse is released.
    - Rectangle Drawing: Updates or creates a rectangle on the canvas. If a rectangle (self.bbox_rect) already exists, its coordinates are updated; if not, a new rectangle is drawn. This visual representation helps users see the area that will be tracked.

Summary

These methods collectively enhance the GUI's interactivity, allowing users to control the view of the video through zooming and to select objects to track via a graphical interface. The zoom functionality provides flexibility in viewing details, while the bounding box selection is crucial for initiating object tracking in user-defined areas of the video. Together, these interactions make the application versatile and user-friendly, adapting to various user needs in real-time video analysis and tracking scenarios.

NAVIGATING FRAME

```python
def prev_frame(self):
    if self.frame_index > 0:
        self.frame_index -= 1
        self.show_frame()

def next_frame(self):
    if self.video and self.frame_index < len(self.video) - 1:
        self.show_frame()
```

The methods prev_frame() and next_frame() provide navigation functionality for the video playback within your BoostingTracker application, allowing users to manually step through the video frame by frame. This is particularly useful for detailed analysis or when fine control over the video is necessary, such as during the precise setup of tracking parameters or close examination of specific events in the video. Here's how these methods work and integrate into your application:

prev_frame() Method
1. Purpose: Allows the user to move backwards in the video to the previous frame.
2. Operation:

- Frame Index Check: The method first checks if the current frame index is greater than zero, ensuring that there is a previous frame to go back to. This prevents the frame index from going into negative values, which would cause errors when attempting to fetch a frame.
- Index Decrement: If the condition is met, it decrements the frame_index by 1 to point to the previous frame.
- Frame Display: Calls show_frame() to update the display with the newly selected frame. This ensures that any changes in frame selection are immediately reflected on the GUI.

next_frame() Method

1. Purpose: Allows the user to advance to the next frame in the video.
2. Operation:
    - Video and Frame Index Check: Checks that a video is loaded (self.video) and that the current frame_index is less than the total number of frames minus one. This condition ensures that there is a next frame available and prevents the frame index from exceeding the available range of frames, which would result in an "index out of range" error.
    - Index Increment: If the conditions are met, it increments the frame_index by 1 before calling show_frame(). Note that in your provided method, the increment seems to be missing, which should typically be there to move to the next frame. Without this increment, the next_frame method would continuously show the same frame, rather than advancing.
    - Frame Display: Calls show_frame() to display the frame at the new index. This method manages the actual fetching and rendering of the frame data.

Integration and Functionality

These methods enhance the user's ability to interact with the video in a controlled manner, important for applications where frame-by-frame analysis is required. By providing buttons or commands linked to these methods, users can manually control video playback, which is essential for detailed observations and when setting or adjusting tracking parameters in specific frames.

By integrating these methods, your application supports more detailed and user-driven interaction with the video content, essential for tasks such as manual tracking setup, video editing, or detailed motion analysis, making it a valuable tool for users needing precise control over video playback.

SETTING WINDOW TITILE

```
def set_window_title(self):
    if self.file_name:
        self.master.title(f"Object Tracking with Boosting Tracker - {self.file_name}")
        self.master.title_font = ("Helvetica", 16, "bold")
    else:
        self.master.title("Object Tracking with Boosting Tracker")
```

The set_window_title() method in BoostingTracker application is a straightforward yet essential utility function designed to update the window title based on the current state of the video file loaded into the application. This method enhances user experience by providing context-sensitive feedback through the window title, indicating whether a video file is loaded and, if so, displaying its name. Here's a breakdown of how this method works and its implications:

Purpose

The primary purpose of this method is to dynamically set the title of the main application window, which helps users identify the video currently being analyzed and offers a more professional and user-friendly interface.

Functionality

1. Conditional Check: The method starts by checking if self.file_name contains a non-empty string. The presence of a file name indicates that a video file has been successfully loaded into the application.
2. Title Update:
    - If a File is Loaded: When self.file_name is not empty, the window title is set to include both a fixed part ("Object Tracking with Boosting Tracker") and the dynamic part (self.file_name). This is formatted as "Object Tracking with Boosting Tracker - {self.file_name}", which clearly informs the user about the active video file.
    - If No File is Loaded: If self.file_name is empty (indicative of no video currently loaded), the title is set to a default value: "Object Tracking with Boosting Tracker". This default title is useful for indicating the application's purpose even in the absence of a loaded video file.
3. Font Styling (Potential Issue):

    The method includes a line to set self.master.title_font to a specific font style and size. However, it's important to note that this property is not a standard attribute or method supported directly by the tk.Tk() window in Tkinter. If the intent is to style the title bar text directly via Tkinter, this approach might not work as expected and could raise an attribute error. Typically, the styling of the window title bar is managed by the operating system and is not directly modifiable through standard Tkinter properties.

Summary

The set_window_title method effectively communicates the application's state to the user through the window title, enhancing usability and context awareness. However, the attempt to set self.master.title_font may not achieve the intended results and could lead to runtime errors.

This method is a small but crucial part of maintaining a user-friendly interface that keeps the user informed about the application's status and current operations.

CLEARING LIST WIDGET

```python
def clear_listbox(self):
    self.center_listbox.delete(0, tk.END)
```

The clear_listbox() method in BoostingTracker application serves a simple yet important function: it clears all entries from the center_listbox widget. This method is typically used in graphical user interfaces (GUIs) where list boxes are employed to display data dynamically, such as tracking information or log entries. Let's examine its utility and implementation:

Purpose and Functionality

1. Purpose: The primary purpose of the clear_listbox() method is to provide a way to reset or clear the content of the center_listbox(). This is particularly useful in scenarios where the user might want to start a new tracking session without closing and reopening the application or to remove clutter from previous sessions to focus on new data.

2. Functionality: The method calls the delete method on the center_listbox object, which is a standard Tkinter Listbox widget method. The parameters 0 and tk.END specify the range of items to delete:
    - 0: This argument signifies the beginning of the listbox, indicating that deletion should start from the very first item.
    - tk.END: This constant points to the end of the listbox, ensuring that deletion continues through to the last item in the list.

Implementation

1. Simplicity: The method is straightforward and concise, making use of Tkinter's built-in functionality to manage list box content efficiently.
2. Integration: It can be integrated into the GUI as part of a button command or an event handler. For example, you might have a "Reset" or "Clear Data" button in your GUI, which, when clicked, triggers this method to clear the list box.

Conclusion

The clear_listbox() method enhances user control over the application by allowing them to manage the display of dynamic data efficiently. It contributes to a better user experience by providing a simple mechanism to reset part of the application's state without affecting other functionalities. In GUI applications, especially those involving real-time data updates, such features are crucial for maintaining an organized and responsive interface.

ANALYZING HISTOGRAM

```python
def analyze_histogram(self):
    if self.bbox2 is not None and self.video:
        x1, y1, x2, y2 = map(int, self.bbox2)
        if x1 != x2 and y1 != y2:
            try:
                frame = self.video.get_data(self.frame_index)
                # Ensure the bounding box is within the frame boundaries
                h, w, _ = frame.shape
                x1, x2 = max(0, min(x1, w)), max(0, min(x2, w))
                y1, y2 = max(0, min(y1, h)), max(0, min(y2, h))

                # Ensure x1 < x2 and y1 < y2
                x1, x2 = sorted([x1, x2])
                y1, y2 = sorted([y1, y2])

                cropped_frame = frame[y1:y2, x1:x2]
                if cropped_frame.size > 0:
                    cropped_frame = cv2.cvtColor(cropped_frame, cv2.COLOR_BGR2RGB)

                    # Get selected filter from combobox
                    selected_filter = self.filter_combobox.get()
                    # Apply selected filter
                    filtered_frame = self.apply_filter(selected_filter, cropped_frame)

                    self.create_popup_window(filtered_frame)
                    self.display_cropped_image(filtered_frame)
                    self.display_histograms(filtered_frame)
                else:
                    print("Cropped frame is empty.")
            except Exception as e:
                print("Failed to process frame:", e)
        else:
            print("Bounding box dimensions are zero or negative.")
```

The analyze_histogram() method in BoostingTracker class is designed to perform a detailed analysis of a specified region within a video frame. This method is particularly useful for applications that require visual data inspection and analysis, such as color distribution or intensity variations within a tracked object or region. Here's a comprehensive breakdown of how this method operates:

1. Method Functionality Overview
    - Bounding Box Validation: The method first ensures that a valid bounding box (self.bbox2) exists and that a video is loaded. The bounding box should not have zero or negative dimensions, which would imply an invalid selection.
    - Frame Extraction: It fetches the current frame from the video at the specified index.
    - Bounding Box Adjustment: Adjusts the bounding box coordinates to ensure they are within the frame's boundaries to prevent errors when cropping.
    - Cropping: Extracts the region defined by the bounding box from the frame.
    - Filter Application: Applies a selected image filter to the cropped region, enhancing or altering the visual data for more detailed analysis.
    - Visualization: Displays the filtered cropped image and its histograms in a popup window for detailed inspection.
2. Step-by-Step Breakdown
    - Check Bounding Box and Video: It verifies that self.bbox2 is not None and that there is a video loaded (self.video). This ensures that there is data to work with.
    - Validate Dimensions: Confirms that the bounding box dimensions are non-zero and positive by checking x1 != x2 and y1 != y2.
    - Fetch Frame: Retrieves the frame at self.frame_index from the video.
    - Coordinate Clamping and Sorting:
        - Clamping: Adjusts the bounding box coordinates to make sure they do not exceed the frame's dimensions, preventing errors during cropping.
        - Sorting: Ensures the top-left and bottom-right coordinates are correctly ordered (x1 < x2, y1 < y2).

- Crop Frame: Extracts the region defined by the bounding box from the frame, converting the color space from BGR to RGB if necessary (assuming OpenCV's default BGR format is used).
- Filter Application:
    - Retrieves the filter selected by the user from a dropdown menu.
    - Applies the selected filter to the cropped region. This step is crucial as it can help enhance features or reduce noise, making subsequent analyses more effective.
- Popup Window Creation and Display:
    - Creates a popup window to display the results.
    - Displays the filtered cropped image.
    - Calculates and displays histograms of the cropped region, providing visual feedback on the color distribution or intensity levels within the selected area.
- Error Handling: Catches and reports any exceptions that occur during processing, aiding in debugging and ensuring the application does not crash unexpectedly.

This method effectively combines multiple image processing techniques to provide a comprehensive tool for detailed visual data inspection, making it a powerful feature of the BoostingTracker application.

HANDLING MOUSE RELEASE EVENT

```
def on_release(self, event):
    self.analyze_histogram()  # Call analyze_histogram() method when the mouse button is released
```

The on_release() method in BoostingTracker application serves as an event handler that is triggered when the user releases the mouse button after clicking and dragging on the video display canvas. This method is strategically utilized to initiate the analysis of a selected region within the video, specifically targeting the area defined by the user's drag (creating a bounding box during the mouse press and drag actions).

CREATING POPUP WINDOW

```python
def create_popup_window(self, cropped_frame):
    self.popup_window = tk.Toplevel(self.master)
    self.popup_window.title("Cropped Image and Its Histogram")
    self.popup_window.geometry("1500x700")
```

The create_popup_window() method in your BoostingTracker application is designed to create and set up a new top-level window (a secondary window) for displaying detailed information about a cropped image and its histogram analysis. Here's a step-by-step explanation of how this method works:

Step 1: Create a New Top-Level Window

- Function: The method begins by creating a new top-level window using tk.Toplevel(self.master). This creates a new window that is a child of the main application window (self.master), but it functions as a separate window.
- Purpose: This secondary window is used to display additional information that needs more space or a separate display context, such as detailed image analysis results.

Step 2: Set the Window Title

- Function: The title of the popup window is set using self.popup_window.title("Cropped Image and Its Histogram").

- Purpose: This title provides the user with immediate context about the contents and purpose of the popup window, which in this case is dedicated to displaying a cropped image from the video and its corresponding histogram.

Step 3: Define the Window Size
- Function: The geometry of the window is set using self.popup_window.geometry("1500x700"). This defines the size of the window as 1500 pixels wide by 700 pixels high.
- Purpose: Specifying the size of the window ensures that there is sufficient space to display the cropped image and its histograms without overcrowding. This size needs to be large enough to accommodate both the image and the graphical representation of the histogram data.

Summary

The create_popup_window() method effectively sets up a new window as a space dedicated to detailed analysis. This allows users to see enhanced details or results from specific operations without losing context or cluttering the main application interface. By using a separate window, the application can maintain a clean and organized main interface while still offering advanced functionality and detailed data presentation when needed. This method exemplifies a good GUI design practice by segregating detailed information into dedicated windows, which can be particularly useful in applications involving image processing, data analysis, or educational tools where detailed visualizations are essential.

DISPLAYING CROPPED IMAGE

```python
def display_cropped_image(self, cropped_frame):
    cropped_frame_frame = tk.Frame(self.popup_window)
    cropped_frame_frame.pack(side="left")

    cropped_frame_rgb = cv2.cvtColor(cropped_frame, cv2.COLOR_BGR2RGB)
    cropped_img = Image.fromarray(cropped_frame_rgb)
    cropped_img = cropped_img.resize((600, 600))

    cropped_photo = ImageTk.PhotoImage(cropped_img)
    cropped_canvas = tk.Canvas(cropped_frame_frame, width=600, height=600)
    cropped_canvas.pack(side="left", anchor="nw")
    cropped_canvas.create_image(0, 0, anchor="nw", image=cropped_photo)
    cropped_canvas.image = cropped_photo
```

The display_cropped_image() method is designed to visualize a cropped section of a video frame within a newly created popup window in your BoostingTracker application. This method meticulously handles the presentation of the image, converting the image format, resizing, and then displaying it in the GUI. Here's a step-by-step breakdown of how the method works:

Step 1: Create a Frame for the Image
- Function: A new tk.Frame named cropped_frame_frame is created as a container within the popup window (self.popup_window).
- Purpose: This frame serves as a dedicated section within the popup window to host the cropped image, helping to organize the layout, especially when other elements like histograms will also be displayed in the same window.

Step 2: Convert the Image Color Format
- Function: The color format of the cropped image is converted from BGR (Blue, Green, Red), which is typical for OpenCV, to RGB (Red, Green, Blue), which is the format expected by most image display libraries including PIL/Tkinter.

- Purpose: This conversion ensures that the image colors are rendered correctly when displayed in the GUI, as failing to convert could result in incorrectly colored images due to channel misalignment.

Step 3: Resize the Image
- Function: The RGB image is resized to a specific dimension (600x600 pixels) using cropped_img.resize((600, 600)).
- Purpose: Resizing standardizes the display size, making the GUI more uniform and ensuring the image fits well within the designed layout without overloading the window with very large images.

Step 4: Create a PhotoImage Object
- Function: A PhotoImage object (cropped_photo) is created from the resized image using ImageTk.PhotoImage(cropped_img).
- Purpose: This step is crucial as it converts the PIL image format into a format that can be used by Tkinter to display the image on a canvas or other widget.

Step 5: Setup a Canvas and Display the Image
- Function:
    - A tk.Canvas named cropped_canvas is created within cropped_frame_frame(), sized to match the resized image (600x600 pixels).
    - The PhotoImage object (cropped_photo) is displayed on this canvas using cropped_canvas.create_image(0, 0, anchor="nw", image=cropped_photo).
- Purpose: The canvas acts as the actual display surface where the image is placed. Using anchor="nw" ensures that the image is positioned at the top-left corner of the canvas.
- Retention of Image Reference: The image reference (cropped_canvas.image = cropped_photo) is retained to prevent the image from being garbage collected by

Python's memory management, which could otherwise lead to the image not being displayed.

Summary

This method effectively handles the task of preparing and displaying a cropped image within a GUI environment. It encapsulates best practices for image processing and GUI presentation, ensuring the image is correctly processed and displayed with the intended visual fidelity. This method is critical for applications requiring visual inspection and analysis of specific regions within a video frame, providing users with a clear and detailed view of selected areas.

DISPLAYING HISTOGRAM

```python
def display_histograms(self, cropped_frame):
    histograms_frame = tk.Frame(self.popup_window)
    histograms_frame.pack(side="right", padx=20)

    self.display_line_histogram(cropped_frame, histograms_frame)
    self.display_bar_histogram(cropped_frame, histograms_frame)
```

The display_histograms() method in BoostingTracker application is designed to visualize the histograms of a cropped image within a popup window. This method complements the image display by providing a visual representation of the color distribution or intensity levels within the cropped area. Histograms are crucial for detailed analysis in many fields, such as digital image processing, photography, and scientific research, because they help users understand the underlying data distribution. Here's a step-by-step breakdown of how this method functions:

Step 1: Create a Container Frame for Histograms
- Function: A tk.Frame named histograms_frame is created and packed into the self.popup_window, aligned to the right side.
- Purpose: This frame serves as a dedicated container for all histogram-related visualizations. By packing it on the right side, it provides a clear and organized layout in the popup window, distinguishing the histogram section from the image display section.

Step 2: Pack the Histograms Frame
- Function: The histograms_frame is packed with a horizontal padding (padx=20), which adds some space around the frame, enhancing the visual separation and overall aesthetics of the GUI layout.
- Purpose: The padding helps to prevent the histograms from appearing cramped and ensures that there is a visual buffer between different UI components, making the interface more user-friendly and easier to interpret.

Step 3: Display Line Histogram
- Function: The method self.display_line_histogram(cropped_frame, histograms_frame) is called.
- Purpose: This method generates and displays a line-style histogram, which is useful for analyzing the distribution of pixel intensities across different color channels. Line histograms provide a smooth and continuous representation of data, which can be especially helpful for spotting subtle variations in intensity.

Step 4: Display Bar Histogram
- Function: The method self.display_bar_histogram(cropped_frame, histograms_frame) is called.
- Purpose: This method generates and displays a bar-style histogram. Unlike line histograms, bar histograms provide a discrete and segmented representation of

data, making them ideal for seeing exact counts or distributions of pixel values at specific intervals. This style of histogram is particularly useful for analyzing digital images where precise pixel value counts are important.

Integration and Visualization Techniques
- Dual Histogram Types: By displaying both line and bar histograms, the application caters to different analysis needs and preferences. Users can get a quick overview with bar histograms and a detailed gradient with line histograms.
- Flexible GUI Layout: The use of a separate frame for histograms ensures that the layout remains flexible and adaptable. Users can focus on either the image or the histogram data as needed without interference.

Summary
The display_histograms() method effectively utilizes GUI components to enhance the analytical capabilities of the BoostingTracker application. By providing clear, detailed visualizations of histograms, it allows users to perform sophisticated image analysis directly within the application. This functionality is essential for applications where understanding the color and intensity distribution is crucial, such as in photo editing, scientific imaging, or any form of digital media analysis.

DISPLAYING LINE HISTOGRAM

```python
def display_line_histogram(self, cropped_frame, histograms_frame):
    line_histogram_frame = tk.Frame(histograms_frame)
    line_histogram_frame.pack(side="top", pady=10)

    plt.figure(figsize=(12, 4))
    color = ('r', 'g', 'b')
    for i, col in enumerate(color):
```

```
        histr = cv2.calcHist([cropped_frame], [i], None, [256], [0, 256])
        plt.plot(histr, color=col, label=f'Channel {col.upper()}', linewidth=2)
        plt.xlim([0, 256])
    plt.title('Line Histogram')
    plt.xlabel('Pixel Value')
    plt.ylabel('Frequency')
    plt.tight_layout()
    plt.grid(True)
    plt.legend()

    line_histogram_img = self.plot_to_image(plt)
    self.display_histogram_image(line_histogram_frame, line_histogram_img)
```

The display_line_histogram() method in BoostingTracker application is specifically designed to generate and display line histograms for different color channels of a cropped image. This method provides a detailed view of the intensity distribution across each channel, which is crucial for understanding the color characteristics and possible anomalies within the selected region of the image. Here's how this method is structured and functions:

Step-by-Step Breakdown
Step 1: Create a Frame for the Line Histogram

- Function: A tk.Frame named line_histogram_frame is created within the parent histograms_frame.
- Purpose: This frame serves as the specific container for the line histogram. It is packed at the top of the histograms_frame with a vertical padding (pady=10), which helps to visually separate it from other potential content in the histograms_frame, enhancing readability and layout structure.

Step 2: Setup the Histogram Plot

- Function: Utilizes matplotlib to create a figure and plot histograms for each color channel (Red, Green, Blue) of the cropped frame.

- A figure with a specific size (figsize=(12, 4)) is initialized to ensure the plot is adequately visible and proportionally fit within the GUI.
- For each channel, cv2.calcHist is used to calculate the histogram, which is then plotted on the figure using plt.plot, with colors corresponding to each channel and labels indicating the channel.
- The x-axis limits are set from 0 to 256, representing possible pixel values for each color channel in an 8-bit image.

Step 3: Configure Plot Aesthetics
- Aesthetic Configurations:
    - plt.title('Line Histogram') sets the title of the histogram plot.
    - plt.xlabel('Pixel Value') and plt.ylabel('Frequency') label the axes to inform the user about the data dimensions being plotted.
    - plt.tight_layout() adjusts the plot parameters to give a clean layout without overlapping content.
    - plt.grid(True) adds a grid to the plot, improving the readability of the histogram.
    - plt.legend() includes a legend that describes which line corresponds to which color channel, aiding in interpretation.

Step 4: Convert Plot to Image and Display
- Function: Converts the matplotlib plot into an image that can be displayed in a Tkinter interface:
    - line_histogram_img = self.plot_to_image(plt): This method presumably captures the plot as an image, suitable for integration within the Tkinter framework.
- Purpose: Displaying this image in the Tkinter GUI:

- The resulting image is then displayed using another method, self.display_histogram_image(line_histogram_frame, line_histogram_img), which adds the image to the line_histogram_frame.

Integration and User Experience
- Detailed Visualization: The line histogram provides a detailed visual analysis of the intensity distribution across color channels, which can be critical for tasks requiring precise color adjustments or for diagnosing issues within the image.
- Interactive Analysis: By embedding this histogram within a GUI, the method enhances user interaction, allowing for a more engaging and informative analysis experience.
- Educational Tool: Such visual tools are excellent for educational purposes, helping users understand digital image processing concepts like color histograms and their implications.

Summary

The display_line_histogram() method effectively leverages matplotlib for data visualization and integrates these visuals into a Tkinter-based GUI. This method not only supports detailed image analysis but also enhances the overall usability and functionality of the application by providing crucial visual data in an accessible manner.

DISPLAYING BAR HISTOGRAM

```python
    def display_bar_histogram(self, cropped_frame, histograms_frame):
        bar_histogram_frame = tk.Frame(histograms_frame)
        bar_histogram_frame.pack(side="bottom", pady=10)

        plt.figure(figsize=(12, 4))
        color = ('r', 'g', 'b')
        for i, col in enumerate(color):
            hist_range = (0, 256)
            hist_counts, _ = np.histogram(cropped_frame[:, :, i], bins=64, range=hist_range)
            plt.bar(np.arange(64), hist_counts, color=col, alpha=0.7, label=f'Channel {col.upper()}')
            for index, value in enumerate(hist_counts):
                plt.text(index, value + 10, str(int(value)), ha='center', va='bottom', fontsize=9)

        plt.title('Bar Histogram')
        plt.xlabel('Pixel Value')
        plt.ylabel('Frequency')
        plt.xticks(np.linspace(0, 63, num=5), np.linspace(0, 255, num=5, dtype=int))
        # Adjust x-axis ticks
        plt.tight_layout()
        plt.grid(True)
        plt.legend()

        bar_histogram_img = self.plot_to_image(plt)
        self.display_histogram_image(bar_histogram_frame, bar_histogram_img)
```

The display_bar_histogram() method provides an essential visualization tool for the BoostingTracker application by displaying bar histograms for each color channel of a cropped image. This detailed visualization helps in understanding the frequency distribution of pixel intensities, which is crucial for tasks like color correction, image analysis, and quality control. Here's a step-by-step explanation of how this method functions:

Step 1: Create a Frame for the Bar Histogram
- Function: A tk.Frame named bar_histogram_frame is created within the parent histograms_frame.
- Purpose: This frame acts as a container specifically for the bar histogram. It is packed at the bottom of the histograms_frame with vertical padding (pady=10), helping to segregate it visually from other content, such as line histograms or the image display itself.

Step 2: Setup the Histogram Plot
- Function: A new matplotlib figure with a specified size (figsize=(12, 4)) is created to ensure clarity and adequate space for displaying data.
- Histogram Calculation:
  - For each color channel (Red, Green, Blue), a histogram is calculated using NumPy's np.histogram function, which provides the counts of pixel intensities within specified bins.
  - The color image data is accessed channel-wise (cropped_frame[:, :, i]), and histograms are computed with 64 bins spanning the full range of possible pixel values (0-255).

Step 3: Plot Bar Histograms
- Bar Plots: Histogram data for each channel is visualized using plt.bar, with each bar representing a bin and colored appropriately for the channel (red, green, or blue).
- Value Labels: Each bar is annotated with its count value using plt.text, enhancing readability and providing exact data points at a glance.

Step 4: Configure Plot Aesthetics
- Plot Configuration:
  - plt.title('Bar Histogram') sets the plot's title.

- plt.xlabel('Pixel Value') and plt.ylabel('Frequency') define the axes labels.
- plt.xticks() adjustment improves the scale of the x-axis, making it more representative of the actual pixel values across the 64 bins.
- plt.tight_layout() ensures that all plot elements are neatly arranged without overlapping.
- plt.grid(True) adds a grid for easier visualization of data points.
- plt.legend() displays a legend to identify which bars correspond to which color channel.

Step 5: Convert Plot to Image and Display

- Image Conversion:
  - bar_histogram_img = self.plot_to_image(plt), a method that presumably captures the matplotlib plot as an image format compatible with Tkinter.
- Display the Image:
  - self.display_histogram_image(bar_histogram_frame, bar_histogram_img) integrates the histogram image into the previously created frame within the GUI.

Integration and User Experience

- Dual Histogram Display: Providing both line and bar histograms allows users to analyze pixel distributions in different visual formats, catering to varied analytical preferences or requirements.
- Interactive Analysis: By embedding these histograms within the GUI, users can interactively explore the color properties of selected image regions, making the application more engaging and informative.

Summary

The display_bar_histogram() method effectively utilizes powerful visualization libraries (matplotlib and NumPy) to generate meaningful insights into image data, which are then seamlessly integrated into the Tkinter-based GUI. This approach not only enhances the application's functionality but also boosts its usability by providing critical visual data in an accessible and interactive manner. This method is particularly valuable for applications requiring detailed image analysis, such as digital forensics, scientific research, and advanced photo editing.

GENERATING HISTOGRAM IMAGE

```python
def display_histogram_image(self, parent_frame, img):
    histogram_photo = ImageTk.PhotoImage(image=img)
    histogram_canvas = tk.Canvas(parent_frame, width=900, height=300)
    histogram_canvas.pack(side="bottom", anchor="se")
    histogram_canvas.create_image(0, 0, anchor="nw", image=histogram_photo)
    histogram_canvas.image = histogram_photo
```

The display_histogram_image() method in BoostingTracker application is designed to take a generated image and display it within a specific parent frame in the Tkinter GUI. This method plays a critical role in visualizing complex data in an easily accessible graphical format. Here's a detailed breakdown of each step in the method and how it contributes to the overall functionality of the application:

Step-by-Step Explanation

Step 1: Convert Image to PhotoImage

- Function: Convert the image (img), which is presumably a matplotlib plot image or similar, into a PhotoImage object using ImageTk.PhotoImage(image=img).
- Purpose: Tkinter does not natively support displaying images in formats used by data visualization libraries like matplotlib. Converting the image to PhotoImage

makes it compatible with Tkinter, allowing it to be displayed within the application's GUI.

Step 2: Create a Canvas

- Function: A tk.Canvas named histogram_canvas is created within the specified parent_frame. The canvas is configured with specific dimensions (width=900, height=300).
- Purpose: The canvas serves as the drawing surface where the image will be rendered. The size is predetermined to ensure that the histogram image fits neatly into the allocated space, maintaining a consistent layout and design within the GUI.

Step 3: Pack the Canvas

- Function: The canvas is packed into the parent_frame using pack(side="bottom", anchor="se").
- Purpose: This packing arrangement places the canvas at the bottom of the parent frame, anchored to the southeast (se). This positioning helps in organizing content within the window, especially when multiple visual elements are present, such as in the case of displaying multiple histograms or additional analytical data.

Step 4: Display the Image on the Canvas

- Function: The histogram image is placed onto the canvas using histogram_canvas.create_image(0, 0, anchor="nw", image=histogram_photo).
- Purpose: This function actually renders the image onto the canvas, with the image anchored at the northwest (nw) corner of the canvas. This ensures that the image aligns correctly at the top-left of the canvas area, providing a clear and unobstructed view.

Step 5: Ensure Image Persistence
- Function: The image reference is stored in the canvas object itself (histogram_canvas.image = histogram_photo).
- Purpose: This step is crucial because Tkinter does not automatically retain a reference to the PhotoImage objects. By storing a reference directly in the canvas, it prevents the Python garbage collector from prematurely clearing the image memory while it's still needed for display. This ensures that the image remains visible for the duration of its necessity in the GUI.

Integration and User Experience

This method enhances the user experience by seamlessly integrating complex data visualizations into the GUI, making the application both functional and user-friendly. By displaying histograms and similar images clearly and effectively, it supports detailed data analysis directly within the application's interface, which is essential for applications involving image processing, statistical data analysis, and educational tools where visual representation of data is crucial.

Summary

The display_histogram_image() method is a vital component of the GUI functionality in the BoostingTracker application, enabling the effective display of graphical data. It showcases how application developers can integrate complex visualizations into practical application scenarios, thereby enhancing both the analytical capabilities and the overall usability of the application.

GENERATING HISTOGRAM BAR IMAGE

```python
    def plot_histogram_bar_to_image(self, image):
        # Calculate histogram for each channel
        histograms = []
        for i in range(3):
            hist_range = (0, 256)
            hist_counts, _ = np.histogram(image[:, :, i], bins=64, range=hist_range)  # Adjust bins to 64
            histograms.append(hist_counts)

        # Extracting only 64 bins from the histogram
        num_bins = 64  # Adjusted to 64 bins

        # Generating colors for each channel
        colors = ['red', 'green', 'blue']

        plt.figure()
        for i, histogram in enumerate(histograms):
            # Normalize the histogram counts for better visualization
            hist_counts = histogram / np.sum(histogram)
            # Setting the color for each channel
            plt.bar(np.arange(num_bins), hist_counts[:num_bins], color=colors[i], alpha=0.7, label=f'Channel {["Red", "Green", "Blue"][i]}')

        plt.xlabel('Pixel Value')
        plt.ylabel('Normalized Frequency')
        plt.title('RGB Channel Histograms')
        plt.grid(True)
        plt.tight_layout()
        plt.legend()

        # Convert the histogram bar graph to an image
        histogram_bar_img = self.plot_to_image(plt)
        histogram_bar_photo = ImageTk.PhotoImage(image=histogram_bar_img)

        return histogram_bar_photo
```

The plot_histogram_bar_to_image() method is a detailed function aimed at visualizing the color distribution in an image through histograms for each color channel and converting this visualization into an image format that can be displayed within a Tkinter GUI. Here's a breakdown of each part of the method and how they function together:

Step-by-Step Explanation

Step 1: Calculate Histograms for Each Color Channel

- Function: Using NumPy's np.histogram function, the method calculates histograms for each of the three color channels (red, green, blue) of the input image.
- Details:
    - The method iterates over the three channels of the image.
    - It computes the histogram for each channel within the range of 0 to 255 and uses 64 bins for the computation, which simplifies the distribution into manageable chunks.
- Purpose: Histograms are crucial for analyzing the intensity distribution across different color channels, which can help in tasks such as color correction, brightness adjustments, or simply understanding the image's color composition.

Step 2: Normalize Histogram Counts

- Function: Normalizes the histogram data to represent frequency as a proportion of the total number of pixels, rather than raw counts. This makes the histogram independent of image size, focusing solely on the distribution pattern.
- Details:
    - Normalization is done by dividing the histogram counts by the total sum of counts, ensuring that the sum of the normalized histogram equals 1.

Step 3: Plot Histograms

- Function: Uses matplotlib to plot the normalized histograms as bar graphs for each color channel.
- Details:
    - Colors for the bars are set to match their respective channels: red, green, and blue.

- The bars are plotted with a slight transparency (alpha set to 0.7) to visually distinguish overlapping areas among the channels.
- Purpose: Visualizing the histograms as bar graphs provides a clear and intuitive understanding of the color intensity distribution. This is especially useful for photographic analysis, image processing education, and debugging image manipulation algorithms.

Step 4: Configure Plot Aesthetics

- Function: Enhances the readability and presentation of the plot with labels, title, grid, and a legend.
- Details:
    - Labels for the x-axis (Pixel Value) and y-axis (Normalized Frequency) clearly define what the axes represent.
    - A grid is enabled to enhance readability of the histograms.
    - A legend is added to help users identify which histogram corresponds to which color channel.

Step 5: Convert the Plot to an Image

- Function: Converts the matplotlib plot to an image format that can be used within Tkinter.
- Details:
    - Calls a utility function self.plot_to_image(plt), which presumably captures the plot as an image, making it suitable for GUI integration.
    - Purpose: This conversion is necessary because Tkinter cannot directly display matplotlib figures. The image needs to be in a format that Tkinter understands (i.e., a PhotoImage object).

Step 6: Create PhotoImage and Return

- Function: Converts the image into a PhotoImage object.

- Purpose: PhotoImage is the format required by Tkinter to display images on widgets like labels or canvases.

Integration and Usage

This method effectively bridges data visualization tools (matplotlib) with a GUI framework (Tkinter), allowing users to interactively explore image data through graphical representations. By providing a method to visualize and display histograms directly in the application, it enhances the analytical capabilities of the software, making it suitable for a wide range of applications in digital image processing, educational tools, or any scenario where understanding the color makeup of images is essential.

CONVERTING MATPLOTLIB INTO IMAGE

```
def plot_to_image(self, plt):
    plt.savefig('temp_plot.png')
    img = Image.open('temp_plot.png')
    return img
```

The plot_to_image() method in BoostingTracker application serves a crucial function by converting matplotlib plots into a format that can be displayed within the Tkinter GUI environment. This method bridges the gap between generating visual data analyses (like histograms) and displaying those results in a graphical user interface. Here's a detailed examination of how this method operates:

Functionality and Steps
Step 1: Save the Plot to a File
- Function: The method uses matplotlib's savefig function to save the current plot to a temporary file named 'temp_plot.png'.

- Purpose: This step captures the visual representation of data (e.g., a histogram) as a static image file. Saving the plot as a file is a straightforward way to convert the plot from an in-memory object to a more usable image format.

Step 2: Open the Image File
- Function: Opens the saved image file using PIL's Image.open, which loads the 'temp_plot.png' file back into Python as an image object.
- Purpose: This operation transitions the image from a disk-based file back into programmatic control, allowing further manipulation or display within the application.

Step 3: Return the Image Object
- Function: Returns the PIL image object to the caller.
- Purpose: The image object can now be manipulated or displayed within the application's GUI, specifically with Tkinter, which supports displaying images via the PhotoImage or similar wrappers.

APPLYING FILTERS

```python
def apply_filter(self, filter_name, frame):
    if filter_name == "None":
        return frame
    elif filter_name == "Gaussian":
        return cv2.GaussianBlur(frame, (5, 5), 0)
    elif filter_name == "Mean":
        return cv2.blur(frame, (5, 5))
    elif filter_name == "Median":
        return cv2.medianBlur(frame, 5)
    elif filter_name == "Bilateral Filtering":
        return cv2.bilateralFilter(frame, 9, 75, 75)
    elif filter_name == "Non-local Means Denoising":
        return cv2.fastNlMeansDenoisingColored(frame, None, 10, 10, 7, 21)
    elif filter_name == "Anisotropic Diffusion":
```

```
        return self.anisotropic_diffusion(frame)
elif filter_name == "Total Variation Denoising":
        return self.total_variation_denoising(frame)
elif filter_name == "Wiener Filter":
        return self.wiener_filter(frame)
elif filter_name == "Adaptive Thresholding":
        return self.adaptive_threshold_each_channel(frame)
elif filter_name == "Haar Wavelet Transform":
        return self.haar_wavelet_transform(frame)
elif filter_name == "Daubechies Wavelet Transform":
        return self.daubechies_wavelet_transform(frame)
else:
        return frame  # Default: return original frame if filter not found
```

The apply_filter() method in BoostingTracker application is a comprehensive function designed to apply various image processing filters to frames based on user selection. This function is crucial for enhancing the video or image data visually or preparing the data for better analysis or tracking accuracy. Here's an overview of how this method operates, along with detailed explanations for each filter type it supports:

Overview

The method takes two parameters: filter_name, which is a string indicating the type of filter to apply, and frame, which is the image frame to be processed. The method returns the modified frame after applying the selected filter or the original frame if no filter is applied or if the filter name is not recognized.

Filter Implementations

1. None:
   - Function: Directly returns the original frame without any modifications.
   - Use Case: Useful when no filtering is desired or to reset to the original state.
2. Gaussian Blur:

- Function: Applies Gaussian blurring using cv2.GaussianBlur. This filter smooths the image by averaging pixel values with a Gaussian-weighted kernel.
- Parameters: (5, 5) specifies the kernel size, and 0 is the standard deviation in the X and Y directions.
- Use Case: Reduces image noise and detail, commonly used for reducing noise or downsampling an image.

3. Mean:
   - Function: Applies average blurring using cv2.blur.
   - Parameters: (5, 5) specifies the kernel size.
   - Use Case: Similar to Gaussian blur but uses a simple arithmetic mean of surrounding pixels, effective for uniform blur.

4. Median:
   - Function: Applies median blurring using cv2.medianBlur.
   - Parameters: 5 specifies the aperture linear size.
   - Use Case: Highly effective against salt-and-pepper noise in the images.

5. Bilateral Filtering:
   - Function: Applies bilateral filtering using cv2.bilateralFilter, which is an edge-preserving, noise-reducing smoothing filter.
   - Parameters: 9 is the diameter of each pixel neighborhood, 75 is the filter sigma in the color space, and another 75 is the filter sigma in the coordinate space.
   - Use Case: Useful for smoothing images while keeping edges sharp.

6. Non-local Means Denoising:
   - Function: Applies Non-local Means Denoising using cv2.fastNlMeansDenoisingColored.
   - Parameters: Different parameters for controlling the strength and window for comparison.

- Use Case: Effective for removing noise while preserving details, suitable for colored images.

7. Anisotropic Diffusion (not directly available in OpenCV):
    - Function: Custom implementation potentially using Perona-Malik algorithm or similar.
    - Use Case: Edge-preserving smoothing filter often used in image processing to remove noise without blurring edges.

8. Total Variation Denoising:
    - Function: Applies Total Variation Denoising, which often involves iterative methods to minimize the total variation of the image.
    - Use Case: Useful in image de-noising while preserving edges by minimizing the total variation of the image.

9. Wiener Filter:
    - Function: A form of linear filter, it minimizes the mean square error between the estimated random process and the desired process.
    - Use Case: Effective in reducing noise when the signal-to-noise ratio is low.

10. Adaptive Thresholding:
    - Function: Converts the image to a binary image based on local mean around the pixel.
    - Use Case: Useful for images with varying illumination.

11. Haar Wavelet Transform:
    - Function: Applies Haar Wavelet Transform, used for image compression and noise reduction.
    - Use Case: Efficiently captures both frequency and location information.

12. Daubechies Wavelet Transform:
    - Function: Applies Daubechies Wavelet Transform, which is known for its approximation and detail coefficients.

- Use Case: Useful in signal and image processing for its smoothing capabilities.

Summary

The apply_filter() method enables dynamic manipulation of image data through various sophisticated filters, greatly enhancing the application's capabilities in image processing and analysis tasks. By providing a wide range of filtering options, it allows users to adapt the image processing according to specific needs or preferences, making it a versatile tool in the context of video and image analysis. This function exemplifies a modular approach to image processing where the effects of different filters can be directly compared and utilized depending on the application requirements.

DEFINING WIENER FILTER

```python
def wiener_filter(self, frame, kernel_size=(5, 5), noise_var=0.01):
    # Check if frame is None
    if frame is None:
        print("Error: Input frame is None.")
        return None

    # Check if frame is a valid numpy array
    if not isinstance(frame, np.ndarray):
        print("Error: Input frame is not a numpy array.")
        return None

    # Check if frame is an empty array
    if frame.size == 0:
        print("Error: Input frame is empty.")
        return None

    # Check if frame is in BGR color space
    if frame.shape[-1] != 3:
        print("Error: Input frame is not in BGR color space.")
        return None

    # Apply Wiener filter
```

```
        filtered_frame = cv2.medianBlur(frame, kernel_size[0])   # Use kernel_size[0]
as the kernel size
        filtered_frame = cv2.fastNlMeansDenoising(filtered_frame, h=noise_var)
        return filtered_frame
```

Let's break down the method step-by-step to clarify what each part does, and also discuss what adjustments would be needed to implement an actual Wiener filter:

Current Implementation Step-by-Step

Step 1: Validate the Input Frame
- Check if None:
  - The function first checks if the input frame is None. If it is, an error message is printed, and None is returned, halting further execution. This check prevents errors in subsequent operations that assume a valid image object.
- Check if Numpy Array:
  - Next, the method checks if the frame is a numpy array. This is important because the image processing operations that follow require the data to be in a numpy array format. If this check fails, it prints an error and returns None.
- Check if Empty:
  - It then checks if the frame is empty (i.e., it has no size). An empty array would cause errors in processing functions, so this check ensures that there is actual image data to process.
- Check Color Space:
  - Lastly, the method verifies that the frame is in the BGR color space by checking that the last dimension (color channels) has a size of 3. This is essential because the subsequent processing assumes a standard three-channel color image typical in OpenCV.

Step 2: Apply Noise Reduction Techniques
- Median Blurring:

- The method applies a median blur to the frame using cv2.medianBlur. The kernel size used for the blurring is the first element of the kernel_size tuple. Median blurring is effective at removing salt-and-pepper noise and does not assume any underlying noise model.
- Non-local Means Denoising:
    - After median blurring, the frame undergoes non-local means denoising via cv2.fastNlMeansDenoising, which uses a specified noise variance (noise_var). This method works by comparing all patches in the image and averaging similar ones, which effectively reduces noise while preserving edges.

Return the Processed Frame

The frame, now denoised using these two methods, is returned. This frame should have less noise compared to the input, ideally making it clearer and of better quality for further processing or analysis.

DEFINING ADAPTIVE THRESHOLD FILTER

```
def adaptive_threshold_each_channel(self, frame):
    # Split the frame into individual channels
    b, g, r = cv2.split(frame)

    # Apply adaptive thresholding to each channel separately
    b_thresh = cv2.adaptiveThreshold(b, 255, cv2.ADAPTIVE_THRESH_GAUSSIAN_C, cv2.THRESH_BINARY, 11, 2)
    g_thresh = cv2.adaptiveThreshold(g, 255, cv2.ADAPTIVE_THRESH_GAUSSIAN_C, cv2.THRESH_BINARY, 11, 2)
    r_thresh = cv2.adaptiveThreshold(r, 255, cv2.ADAPTIVE_THRESH_GAUSSIAN_C, cv2.THRESH_BINARY, 11, 2)

    # Merge the thresholded channels back together
    return cv2.merge([b_thresh, g_thresh, r_thresh])
```

The adaptive_threshold_each_channel() method applies adaptive thresholding separately to each color channel of an image frame and then merges the results back into a single image. This approach can be particularly useful for handling images with varying lighting conditions across the image, enhancing the visibility of features in each channel independently. Here's a detailed explanation of how this method functions:

Step-by-Step Breakdown

Step 1: Split the Frame into Individual Channels
- Function: cv2.split(frame) is used to divide the input image frame into its three primary color channels: blue (b), green (g), and red (r).
- Purpose: By splitting the image into individual color channels, the method can apply adaptive thresholding to each channel separately. This is important because different channels may have different lighting conditions and feature visibility.

Step 2: Apply Adaptive Thresholding to Each Channel
- Function: Adaptive thresholding is applied to each channel using OpenCV's cv2.adaptiveThreshold. This function takes several parameters:
  - src: The source image, which is one of the color channels in this case.
  - maxValue: The maximum intensity value to use, set to 255, which is the maximum value for an 8-bit image.
  - adaptiveMethod: Specifies the adaptive method to calculate the threshold for each pixel neighborhood. cv2.ADAPTIVE_THRESH_GAUSSIAN_C computes a threshold based on a weighted sum of the local neighborhood minus a constant (in this case, 2), where weights are a Gaussian window.
  - thresholdType: The type of thresholding, which here is cv2.THRESH_BINARY, meaning each pixel will be set to the maximum value if the resulting threshold is exceeded.

- blockSize: The size of the local region to calculate the threshold, set to 11, which determines the area around each pixel used for calculating its threshold.
- C: A constant subtracted from the mean or weighted sum of the neighborhood pixels. Here it is 2, which adjusts the calculated threshold slightly for each pixel.
- Purpose: Adaptive thresholding adjusts the threshold dynamically for different areas of the image based on the local pixel intensity distributions. This helps in compensating for different lighting conditions across the image, making it particularly effective for images with shadows or illumination gradients.

Step 3: Merge the Thresholded Channels Back Together
- Function: cv2.merge([b_thresh, g_thresh, r_thresh]) combines the separately processed channels back into a single image.
- Purpose: After processing, the individual binary images for each channel are combined to form a single three-channel image where each channel has been thresholded according to its specific characteristics. This results in an image that can exhibit more defined and separated features based on lighting and color variations.

Practical Usage and Implications
- Enhanced Feature Detection: This method is especially useful for scenarios where distinct features need to be enhanced or isolated in images with uneven lighting or diverse color profiles.
- Pre-processing for Image Analysis: It can serve as a pre-processing step for further image analysis tasks, such as object detection, where clear distinctions between features and the background are necessary.

- Visual Effects: In artistic or creative contexts, this method can be used to create a stark, graphic look by converting images into high-contrast, color-specific binary images.

This method enhances the adaptability of image processing applications to handle complex scenarios with varying image qualities and conditions, providing a robust tool for detailed image analysis and manipulation.

DEFINING HAAR FILTER

```
def haar_wavelet_transform(self, frame):
    # Split the frame into its individual color channels
    b, g, r = cv2.split(frame)

    # Perform the wavelet transform on each channel separately
    b_coeffs = pywt.dwt2(b, 'haar')
    g_coeffs = pywt.dwt2(g, 'haar')
    r_coeffs = pywt.dwt2(r, 'haar')

    # Reconstruct the channels from the coefficients
    b_reconstructed = pywt.idwt2(b_coeffs, 'haar')
    g_reconstructed = pywt.idwt2(g_coeffs, 'haar')
    r_reconstructed = pywt.idwt2(r_coeffs, 'haar')

    # Clip the values to ensure they are within the valid range
    b_reconstructed = np.clip(b_reconstructed, 0, 255).astype(np.uint8)
    g_reconstructed = np.clip(g_reconstructed, 0, 255).astype(np.uint8)
    r_reconstructed = np.clip(r_reconstructed, 0, 255).astype(np.uint8)

    # Merge the channels back together
    return cv2.merge([b_reconstructed, g_reconstructed, r_reconstructed])
```

The haar_wavelet_transform() method in BoostingTracker application uses the Haar wavelet transform for each color channel of an image, performs a decomposition and then a reconstruction of the image data. This approach is utilized typically for applications like image compression, feature extraction, and noise reduction. Here's a step-by-step breakdown of how the method operates and its significance:

Step-by-Step Breakdown

Step 1: Split the Frame into Individual Color Channels
- Function: cv2.split(frame) separates the input image frame into its three primary color channels: blue (b), green (g), and red (r).
- Purpose: Splitting the image into individual channels allows for separate processing on each channel, which is necessary because the wavelet transform will treat each channel's data independently.

Step 2: Perform the Haar Wavelet Transform
- Function: pywt.dwt2 is used on each channel to perform the discrete wavelet transform using the Haar wavelet.
- dwt2 stands for two-dimensional discrete wavelet transform, which decomposes the image into four sub-bands: LL (low-low), LH (low-high), HL (high-low), and HH (high-high). Here, 'haar' specifies the type of wavelet used.
- Purpose: The Haar wavelet transform provides a simple and computationally efficient way to decompose the image into different frequency components, capturing both spatial and frequency information. This is useful for analyzing the image at different scales and resolutions.

Step 3: Reconstruct the Channels from the Wavelet Coefficients
- Function: pywt.idwt2 is used for the inverse discrete wavelet transform, which reconstructs the original data from the wavelet coefficients.
- Purpose: After analyzing or processing the coefficients (not explicitly shown in your code but typical in applications using wavelet transforms), the inverse transform reconstructs the image channels. This step is essential to recombine the modified frequency components back into a spatial representation.

Step 4: Clip the Values and Convert to 8-bit Unsigned Integers

- Function: np.clip is used on each reconstructed channel to ensure pixel values remain within the valid range for image data (0-255), followed by conversion to np.uint8 to ensure the image format is suitable for display and further processing.
- Purpose: Clipping and converting the data type ensures that no overflow or underflow occurs due to transformations, which might otherwise lead to visual artifacts or errors in the image data.

Step 5: Merge the Channels Back Together

- Function: cv2.merge([b_reconstructed, g_reconstructed, r_reconstructed]) recombines the individually processed color channels into a single three-channel image.
- Purpose: Merging the channels restores the full color image, allowing it to be displayed or further processed as a standard BGR image used in many CV applications.

Practical Usage and Benefits

- Image Compression: By manipulating the wavelet coefficients before reconstruction, you can achieve effective image compression, which is useful in reducing storage requirements or bandwidth for transmission.
- Noise Reduction: Selective thresholding or modification of the wavelet coefficients can effectively reduce image noise while preserving important details, making this method useful in preprocessing steps for image analysis or computer vision tasks.
- Feature Extraction: The multi-resolution nature of wavelet transforms makes them suitable for extracting features from images that are useful in various image processing and machine learning applications.

Conclusion

The method effectively uses the Haar wavelet transform to decompose and then reconstruct an image, which can be adapted for various advanced image processing tasks. By manipulating the wavelet coefficients between the decomposition and reconstruction steps (not covered in the provided code but typically done in practical applications), significant enhancements and modifications can be applied to the image data.

DEFINING DAUBECHIES FILTER

```python
def daubechies_wavelet_transform(self, frame):
    # Split the frame into its individual color channels
    b, g, r = cv2.split(frame)

    # Choose the wavelet function (Daubechies 5)
    wavelet = 'db5'

    # Perform the wavelet transform on each channel separately
    b_coeffs = pywt.dwt2(b, wavelet)
    g_coeffs = pywt.dwt2(g, wavelet)
    r_coeffs = pywt.dwt2(r, wavelet)

    # Reconstruct the channels from the coefficients
    b_reconstructed = pywt.idwt2(b_coeffs, wavelet)
    g_reconstructed = pywt.idwt2(g_coeffs, wavelet)
    r_reconstructed = pywt.idwt2(r_coeffs, wavelet)

    # Clip the values to ensure they are within the valid range
    b_reconstructed = np.clip(b_reconstructed, 0, 255).astype(np.uint8)
    g_reconstructed = np.clip(g_reconstructed, 0, 255).astype(np.uint8)
    r_reconstructed = np.clip(r_reconstructed, 0, 255).astype(np.uint8)

    # Merge the channels back together
    return cv2.merge([b_reconstructed, g_reconstructed, r_reconstructed])
```

The daubechies_wavelet_transform() method processes an image using the Daubechies wavelet, specifically the "db5" wavelet, which is known for its good performance in various signal and image processing tasks due to its ability to compactly represent data and preserve higher moments of datasets. This function effectively decomposes each color channel of the image, applies the wavelet transform, and then reconstructs the channels, aiming to potentially enhance or alter the image characteristics. Let's break down the steps and discuss each one in detail:

Step-by-Step Breakdown
Step 1: Split the Frame into Individual Color Channels
- Function: Uses cv2.split(frame) to separate the input frame into its blue (b), green (g), and red (r) components.
- Purpose: Splitting the image into individual channels is essential for processing each color component separately with the wavelet transform, which can yield different results depending on the color channel due to varying information content in each.

Step 2: Select the Wavelet Function
- Function: Defines wavelet = 'db5', specifying the Daubechies wavelet of order 5.
- Purpose: The 'db5' wavelet is chosen for its properties, which include five vanishing moments making it more accurate and smooth for image processing. It provides a good balance between spatial and frequency resolution.

Step 3: Perform Wavelet Transform on Each Channel
- Function: Applies pywt.dwt2 to each channel. This function performs a two-dimensional discrete wavelet transform.
- Purpose: The wavelet transform decomposes each channel into a low-frequency approximation (useful for image analysis and feature extraction) and high-frequency details (capturing edges and other fine image details).

Step 4: Reconstruct Channels from Wavelet Coefficients

- Function: Uses pywt.idwt2 to reconstruct each channel from its wavelet coefficients.
- Purpose: This inverse transform rebuilds the original data from the wavelet coefficients, potentially after modifications for applications such as noise reduction, compression, or feature enhancement.

Step 5: Clip and Convert the Values

- Function: Applies np.clip to each reconstructed channel to ensure pixel values remain within the standard 8-bit range (0-255), followed by conversion to type np.uint8.
- Purpose: Clipping and type conversion ensure that the image data remains valid for display and further processing, preventing issues like overflow or underflow which can distort the image.

Step 6: Merge Channels Back Together

- Function: Combines the processed channels back into a single image using cv2.merge([b_reconstructed, g_reconstructed, r_reconstructed]).
- Purpose: Reintegrating the channels restores the full-color image, allowing it to be used in subsequent processing or displayed as part of the application's output.

Practical Usage and Implications

- Noise Reduction: By manipulating the wavelet coefficients (especially by thresholding or modifying high-frequency components), this method can effectively reduce noise while preserving essential details.
- Image Compression: Wavelet transforms, due to their hierarchical nature, are excellent for image compression, allowing high-quality reconstruction from compressed data.

- Feature Extraction: The low-frequency components from wavelet transforms are useful for extracting features that are robust to variations in image scale and orientation.

Conclusion

This method efficiently uses the Daubechies wavelet to enhance or modify image characteristics, making it valuable for advanced image processing tasks. Its application in the BoostingTracker enhances the tool's capabilities, especially in environments where image quality and detail are paramount.

DEFINING ANISOTROPIC DIFFUSION

```
def anisotropic_diffusion(self, img):
    return cv2.fastNlMeansDenoisingColored(img, None, 10, 10, 7, 21)
```

The anisotropic_diffusion() method is intended to perform noise reduction on an image, but there appears to be a semantic error in naming and functionality. The method uses OpenCV's cv2.fastNlMeansDenoisingColored, which is actually an implementation of the Non-Local Means Denoising algorithm, not anisotropic diffusion. Here's a breakdown of how this function works and some context on actual anisotropic diffusion:

Explanation of Non-Local Means Denoising

1. Function: cv2.fastNlMeansDenoisingColored(img, None, 10, 10, 7, 21)
   - img: The input color image.
   - None: Placeholder for a mask which isn't used in this case.
   - 10: The "h" parameter, controlling the filter strength. Higher values remove noise more effectively but can also remove image details.

- 10: The "hForColorComponents" parameter, similar to "h" but used for color images.
- 7: Template window size. It affects performance and how much the surrounding pixels contribute to the denoising process.
- 21: Search window size. Determines how far the algorithm will search for patches to compare.

2. Purpose: This function reduces noise across the image by comparing each patch of the image with other patches in a larger search area and averaging similar patches. This effectively reduces the noise while preserving the structural details in the image, making it well-suited for high-quality photography and other applications requiring preservation of fine details without the noise.

APPLYING TOTAL VARIATION DENOISING

```python
def apply_total_variation_denoising_channel(self, channel, weight, iterations):
    # Initialize the result with the original channel
    result = channel.copy().astype(np.float64)  # Convert to float64

    # Perform total variation denoising
    for _ in range(iterations):
        # Compute the gradient of the channel
        dx = cv2.Sobel(result, cv2.CV_64F, 1, 0, ksize=3)
        dy = cv2.Sobel(result, cv2.CV_64F, 0, 1, ksize=3)

        # Update the channel using the gradient and the weight
        result -= weight * np.sqrt(dx**2 + dy**2)

    # Clip the values to ensure they are within the valid range
    result = np.clip(result, 0, 255).astype(np.uint8)

    return result
```

The apply_total_variation_denoising_channel() method provides a way to apply total variation (TV) denoising to a single channel of an image. Total Variation denoising is a popular technique in image processing used to reduce noise while preserving edges by minimizing the total variation of the image. Here's a detailed step-by-step explanation of how this method works:

Step-by-Step Breakdown
Step 1: Initialize the Result
- Function: The method begins by creating a copy of the input channel and converting it to np.float64.
- Purpose: This step ensures that the calculations during the denoising process have sufficient precision. Using float64 is crucial to avoid overflow or underflow during gradient calculations and subsequent operations.

Step 2: Perform Total Variation Denoising
- Iterative Process:
  - The denoising process is iterative, with the number of iterations specified by the iterations parameter.
- Gradient Computation:
  - For each iteration, the method computes the horizontal (dx) and vertical (dy) gradients of the image using the Sobel operator, which is implemented via cv2.Sobel.
  - The Sobel operator is applied with a kernel size of 3, providing a good balance between accuracy and computational efficiency.
- Update Using the Gradient:
  - The image is updated by subtracting a term that depends on the weight (weight) and the magnitude of the gradient (np.sqrt(dx**2 + dy**2)). This update rule encourages regions of the image to become smoother while

preserving sharp edges, as the update magnitude diminishes near edges where the gradient is large.

Step 3: Clip the Values

- Function: After completing all iterations, the pixel values of result are clipped to the range [0, 255] and converted back to np.uint8.
- Purpose: This step ensures that the resulting image can be handled by typical image processing or display functions, which usually expect uint8 data types representing standard 8-bit per channel images.

Technical Insights and Considerations

- Gradient Magnitude Influence: The update term involves the magnitude of the gradient, which acts as a penalization for large changes in pixel values. Where the gradient is small, the image will be smoothed more significantly. Near edges, where the gradient is large, the smoothing effect is reduced, thus preserving edges.
- Weight Parameter: The weight parameter controls the strength of the smoothing. Higher values result in stronger smoothing effects. The appropriate value of weight can vary depending on the characteristics of the input image and the desired level of denoising.
- Iteration Count: The iterations parameter affects how much the denoising process converges towards a solution. More iterations generally lead to smoother images but increase computational time. The optimal number of iterations might depend on the initial noise level and the desired outcome.

Practical Usage

- Image Preprocessing: This method can be particularly useful as a preprocessing step in computer vision pipelines, where noise reduction can help improve the results of subsequent tasks such as feature detection, segmentation, and classification.
- Selective Denoising: Since the method operates on a single channel, it allows for selective denoising of specific channels in color images, which can be useful when different channels exhibit varying noise characteristics.

Conclusion

The apply_total_variation_denoising_channel() method efficiently implements a fundamental technique in image denoising, providing a versatile tool for improving image quality in noise-affected scenarios while preserving important structural details such as edges. This method is a valuable addition to any image processing toolkit, suitable for both research and practical applications in various fields of image analysis and computer vision.

DEFINING TOTAL VARIATION DENOISING

```
def total_variation_denoising(self, img, weight=0.01, iterations=20):
    # Split the image into its individual color channels
    b, g, r = cv2.split(img)

    # Apply total variation denoising to each channel separately
    b_denoised = self.apply_total_variation_denoising_channel(b, weight, iterations)
    g_denoised = self.apply_total_variation_denoising_channel(g, weight, iterations)
    r_denoised = self.apply_total_variation_denoising_channel(r, weight, iterations)

    # Merge the denoised channels back together
```

```
return cv2.merge([b_denoised, g_denoised, r_denoised])
```

The total_variation_denoising() method processes a color image by applying total variation denoising to each of its color channels (blue, green, and red) independently and then merging the results. This method is based on the principle of total variation reduction, which is effective for noise removal while preserving edges, making it highly suitable for various image processing applications where maintaining edge integrity is crucial. Let's walk through the method step-by-step:

Step-by-Step Breakdown
Step 1: Split the Image into Individual Color Channels
- Function: The image img is split into its three primary color channels using cv2.split(img).
- Purpose: By separating the image into color channels, the method can apply denoising techniques to each channel independently. This is particularly useful because noise characteristics and intensity may differ across channels, and separate processing allows tailored noise reduction.

Step 2: Apply Total Variation Denoising to Each Channel
- Function: The method apply_total_variation_denoising_channel is called for each channel with specified parameters for weight and iterations.
  - b_denoised: Applies denoising to the blue channel.
  - g_denoised: Applies denoising to the green channel.
  - r_denoised: Applies denoising to the red channel.
- Parameters:
  - weight: Controls the denoising strength. Higher values lead to stronger denoising, which might also blur the image more.

- iterations: Specifies the number of iterations in the denoising process. More iterations can lead to more thorough denoising but at the cost of increased computation time.
- Purpose: Total variation denoising minimizes the total variation of the image, effectively reducing noise while preserving edges. It does this by smoothing areas with small variations in intensity while leaving sharp transitions, like edges, largely intact.

Step 3: Merge the Denoised Channels Back Together
- Function: The denoised channels are recombined into a single image using cv2.merge([b_denoised, g_denoised, r_denoised]).
- Purpose: Merging the independently processed channels reconstructs the full color image. This step is crucial as it restores the structure of the original image format, making it suitable for display or further processing.

Practical Usage and Benefits
- Enhanced Image Quality: This method is particularly beneficial for images captured in low light conditions or where the sensor has introduced significant noise. It enhances image quality by reducing noise while maintaining the sharpness of edges, which is essential for both human perception and further automated image processing tasks.
- Versatile Application: Suitable for applications in medical imaging, satellite image processing, and photography, where maintaining edge detail is vital for accurate interpretation and analysis.
- Preprocessing for Advanced Tasks: Often used as a preprocessing step before performing tasks such as segmentation, feature extraction, or machine learning-based analysis, as cleaner images typically improve the accuracy and effectiveness of such algorithms.

Conclusion

The total_variation_denoising() method effectively harnesses the principles of total variation reduction to improve image quality comprehensively across all color channels. By handling each channel individually, it allows for nuanced adjustments to denoising, accommodating the unique characteristics of each channel. This method provides a powerful tool for enhancing image clarity and detail, making it a valuable addition to any advanced image processing or computer vision toolkit.

ENTRY POINT FOR APPLICATION

```
def main():
    root = tk.Tk()
    app = BoostingTracker(root)
    root.mainloop()

if __name__ == "__main__":
    main()
```

The code is the entry point for a typical Tkinter application that uses a custom class named BoostingTracker. This setup is standard for starting GUI applications in Python using the Tkinter library. Let me walk you through what each part of the code does and how it sets up and runs the GUI application:

Detailed Breakdown of the Main Function

Step 1: Create the Main Application Window

- Function: root = tk.Tk()
- tk.Tk(): This is a constructor of the Tk class from the Tkinter module (tk). It creates the main window of the application. This window (root) serves as the primary container for all other GUI components (widgets) and sets the context in which the GUI operates.

Step 2: Initialize the Custom Application Class
- Function: app = BoostingTracker(root)
  - BoostingTracker(root): This line initializes an instance of the BoostingTracker class, passing the root window as an argument. The BoostingTracker class is presumably defined elsewhere in your codebase and should inherit from some form of Tkinter widget or utilize Tkinter widgets within it.
  - Purpose: The BoostingTracker is likely a complex widget or set of widgets configured specifically for tracking objects, possibly in video or image sequences, which requires user interaction and visualization.

Step 3: Enter the Tkinter Main Event Loop
- Function: root.mainloop()
  - mainloop(): This method is crucial as it starts the Tkinter event loop. In GUI programming, the event loop is responsible for handling events such as button clicks, mouse movements, keyboard presses, or system messages. This loop runs continuously until the application window is closed.
  - Purpose: Without calling mainloop(), the application window would open and close immediately because the script would terminate. mainloop() keeps the program running, waiting for user interactions and responding accordingly.

Execution Context

if __name__ == "__main__":

This conditional statement checks if the script is being run as the main program. This is a common Python idiom that prevents certain code blocks from running when the script is imported as a module in another script. Here, it ensures that the Tkinter application only starts when this script is executed directly, not when imported.

Use and Modification

This setup is standard for Tkinter applications, allowing for straightforward modifications and enhancements. You can easily add functionality to the BoostingTracker class, modify how the application is initialized, or handle different events by expanding the code inside the BoostingTracker class or the main function.

This basic structure forms the backbone of many Python-based GUI applications, providing a clear and manageable way to structure the application for effective user interaction and functionality.

RUNNING PROGRAM

Run program and choose certain frame by pushing Next Frame button. Then, draw a bounding box rectangle on certain object in the frame and push Next Frame button.

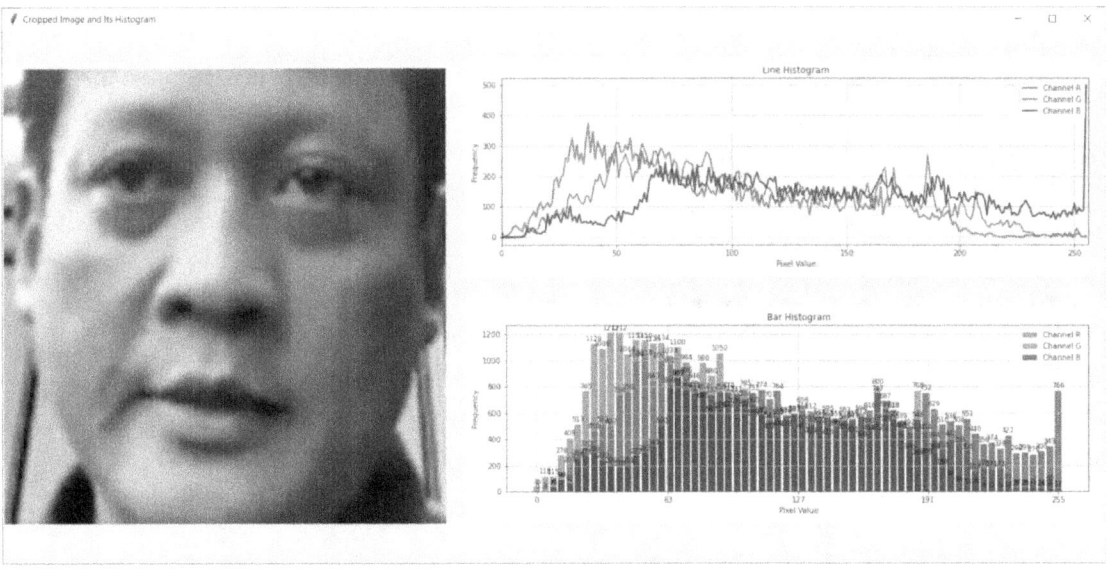

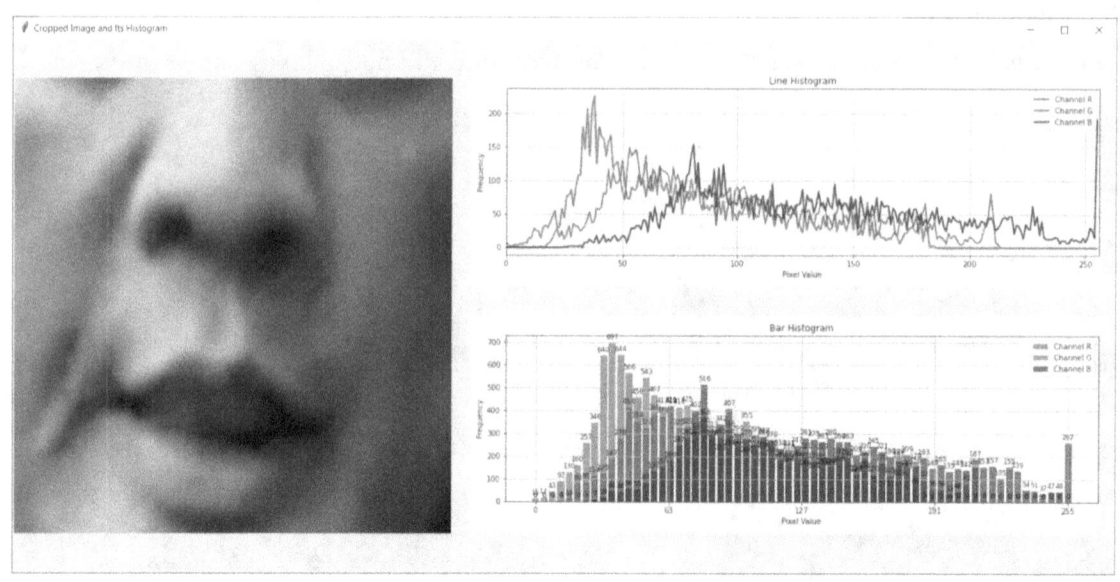

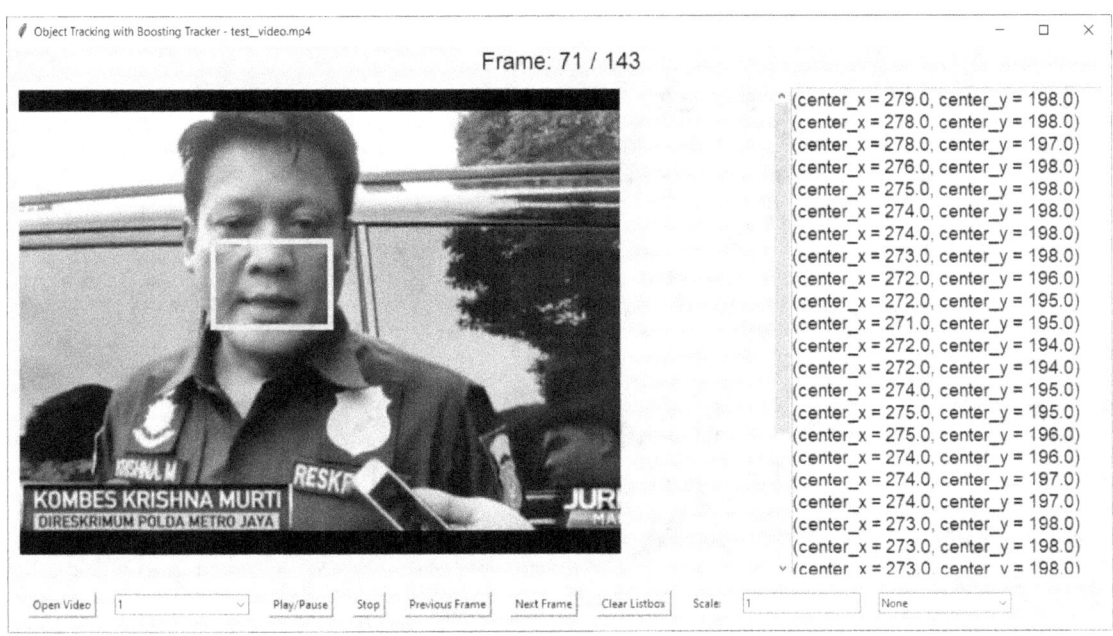

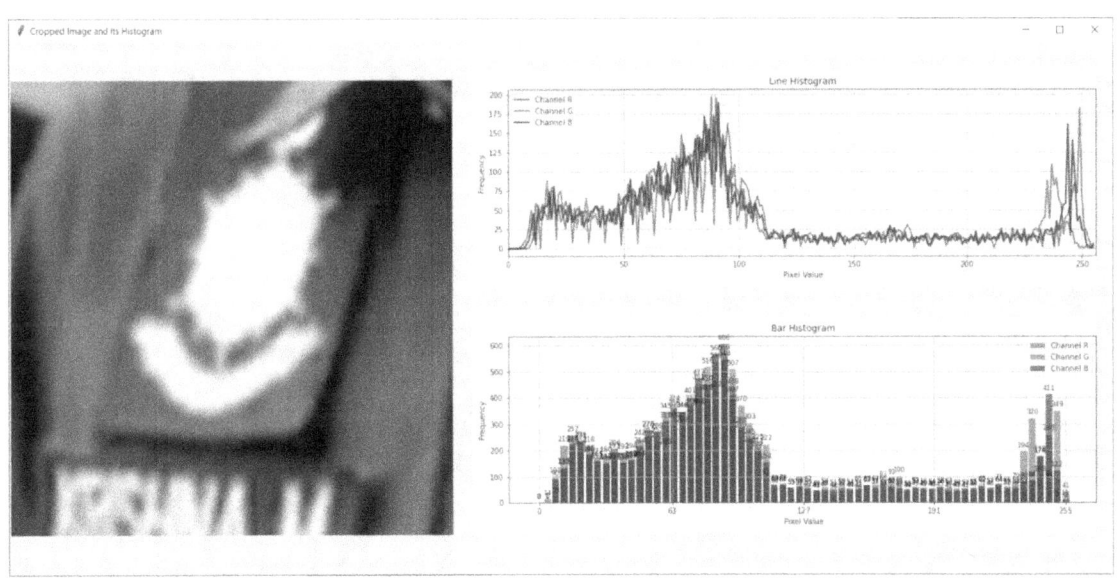

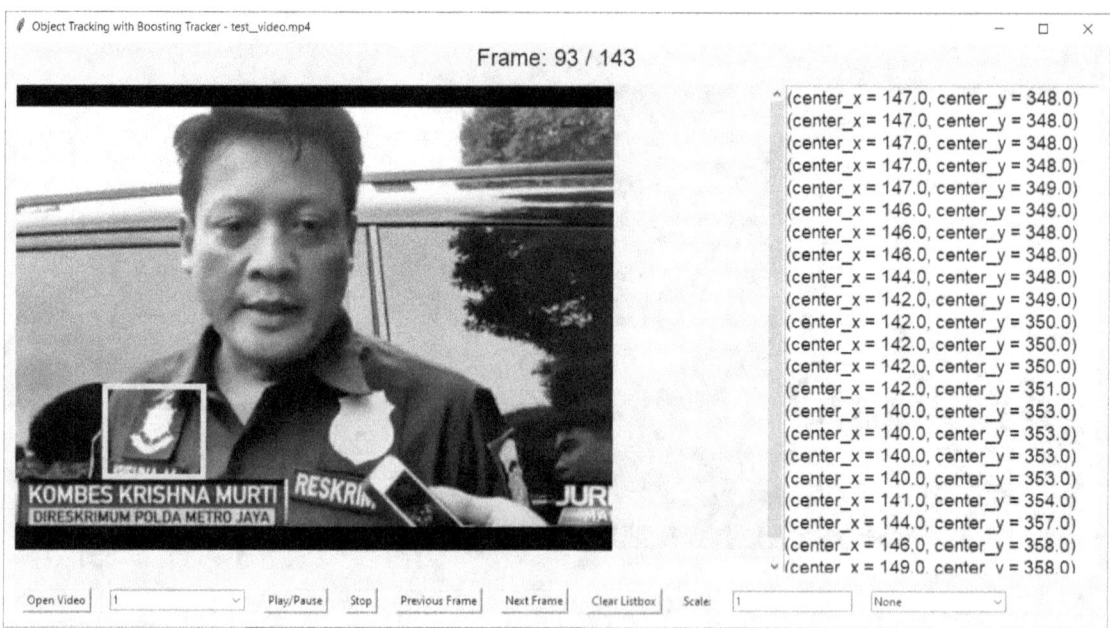

SOURCE CODE

```
#boosting_tracker.py
import tkinter as tk
from tkinter import ttk
from tkinter import filedialog
from PIL import Image, ImageTk
import imageio
import cv2
import numpy as np
import matplotlib.pyplot as plt
import pywt

class BoostingTracker:
    def __init__(self, master):
        self.master = master
        self.master.title("Object Tracking with Boosting Tracker")
        self.file_name = ""
        self.set_window_title()  # Set window title initially

        self.frame_number_label = tk.Label(master, text="Frame: 0")
        self.frame_number_label.pack()
```

```python
        self.video = None
        self.video_path = None
        self.paused = False
        self.zoom_scale = tk.IntVar(value=1)
        self.frame_index = 0
        self.bbox = None
        self.bbox2 = None
        self.tracking_started = False  # Initialize tracking_started to False
        self.prev_frame_gray = None
        self.tracker = None
        self.initial_w = None
        self.initial_h = None
        self.bbox_rect = None  # Initialize bbox_rect attribute to None
        self.frame_processing = False  # Initialize frame_processing attribute to
False

        # Available filters
        self.filters = ["None", "Gaussian", "Mean", "Median", "Bilateral Filtering",
                    "Non-local Means Denoising", "Anisotropic Diffusion",
                    "Total Variation Denoising", "Wiener Filter",
                    "Adaptive Thresholding", "Haar Wavelet Transform",
                    "Daubechies Wavelet Transform"]

        self.create_widgets()

    def create_widgets(self):
        # Panel for video display
        video_panel = tk.Frame(self.master)
        video_panel.pack(padx=10, pady=10)

        # Canvas to display the original video
        canvas_width = 800
        canvas_height = 500
        self.canvas = tk.Canvas(video_panel, width=canvas_width,
height=canvas_height)
        self.canvas.pack(side="left", fill="both", expand=True)
        self.canvas.bind("<MouseWheel>", self.on_mousewheel)
        self.canvas.bind("<ButtonPress-1>", self.on_press)
        self.canvas.bind("<B1-Motion>", self.on_drag)
        self.canvas.bind("<ButtonRelease-1>", self.on_release)  # Bind ButtonRelease
event

        # List box to display center coordinates
        self.center_listbox = tk.Listbox(video_panel, width=30, height=20,
font=("Helvetica", 14))
        self.center_listbox.pack(side="right", fill="y")
        # Scrollbar for the listbox
        scrollbar = tk.Scrollbar(video_panel, orient="vertical")
```

```python
        scrollbar.pack(side="left", fill="y")
        scrollbar.config(command=self.center_listbox.yview)

        # Attach scrollbar to listbox
        self.center_listbox.config(yscrollcommand=scrollbar.set)

        # Panel for control buttons
        control_panel = tk.Frame(self.master)
        control_panel.pack(padx=10, pady=(0, 10), fill="x")

        # Button to open a video file
        self.open_button = tk.Button(control_panel, text="Open Video", command=self.open_video)
        self.open_button.grid(row=0, column=0, padx=10, pady=5)

        # Combobox for selecting zoom scale
        self.zoom_combobox = ttk.Combobox(control_panel, textvariable=self.zoom_scale, values=list(range(1, 11)))
        self.zoom_combobox.grid(row=0, column=1, padx=10, pady=5)
        self.zoom_combobox.bind("<<ComboboxSelected>>", self.update_zoom)

        # Button to play/pause the video
        self.play_button = tk.Button(control_panel, text="Play/Pause", command=self.toggle_play_pause)
        self.play_button.grid(row=0, column=2, padx=10, pady=5)

        # Button to stop the video
        self.stop_button = tk.Button(control_panel, text="Stop", command=self.stop_video)
        self.stop_button.grid(row=0, column=3, padx=10, pady=5)

        # Button to navigate to the previous frame
        self.prev_frame_button = tk.Button(control_panel, text="Previous Frame", command=self.prev_frame)
        self.prev_frame_button.grid(row=0, column=4, padx=10, pady=5)

        # Button to navigate to the next frame
        self.next_frame_button = tk.Button(control_panel, text="Next Frame", command=self.next_frame)
        self.next_frame_button.grid(row=0, column=5, padx=10, pady=5)

        # Button to clear the listbox
        self.clear_button = tk.Button(control_panel, text="Clear Listbox", command=self.clear_listbox)
        self.clear_button.grid(row=0, column=6, padx=10, pady=5)

        # Label and entry for specifying scale
        self.scale_label = tk.Label(control_panel, text="Scale:")
```

```python
        self.scale_label.grid(row=0, column=7, padx=10, pady=5, sticky="e")
        self.scale_default = tk.StringVar(value="1")
        self.scale_entry = ttk.Entry(control_panel, textvariable=self.scale_default)
        self.scale_entry.grid(row=0, column=8, padx=10, pady=5, sticky="w")
        self.scale_entry.bind("<Return>", lambda event: self.toggle_play_pause())

        # Combobox for selecting filters
        self.filter_combobox = ttk.Combobox(control_panel, values=self.filters)
        self.filter_combobox.grid(row=0, column=9, padx=10, pady=5)
        self.filter_combobox.current(0)  # Set default value

    def open_video(self):
        self.video_path = filedialog.askopenfilename(filetypes=[("Video files", "*.mp4;*.avi;*.mkv;*.wmv")])
        if self.video_path:
            self.video = imageio.get_reader(self.video_path)
            self.file_name = self.video_path.split('/')[-1]
            self.set_window_title()
            self.play_video()

    def play_video(self):
        if self.video:
            self.paused = False
            self.tracking_started = True
            self.show_frame()

    def stop_video(self):
        self.paused = True
        self.frame_index = 0
        self.bbox = None
        self.tracker = None  # Reset tracker
        self.initial_w = None  # Reset width
        self.initial_h = None  # Reset height
        self.show_frame()

    def toggle_play_pause(self):
        self.paused = not self.paused
        if not self.paused:
            if self.bbox is not None:
                self.tracking_started = True
            self.play_video()

    def update_zoom(self, event=None):
        self.show_frame()

    def initialize_tracker(self, frame, bbox, params=None):
        """Initialize the tracker with possible user-defined parameters."""
        if params:
```

```python
            # Here you could adjust bbox based on params, if params affect size, etc.
            scale = int(self.scale_entry.get())  # Get threshold from entry
            bbox = (
                bbox[0], bbox[1],
                int(bbox[2] * scale), int(bbox[3] * scale)
            )

        # Initialize the tracker
        self.tracker = cv2.legacy.TrackerBoosting_create()
        self.tracker.init(frame, tuple(map(int, bbox)))
        self.initial_w, self.initial_h = bbox[2], bbox[3]

    def track_object(self, frame, bbox, user_params=None):
        """Track object using Boosting Tracker with optional user parameters."""
        if bbox:
            if self.tracker is None:
                self.initialize_tracker(frame, bbox, user_params)

            # Update the tracker and get the new bounding box
            success, bbox = self.tracker.update(frame)
            if success:
                x1, y1, w, h = map(int, bbox)
                # Use stored initial dimensions
                w, h = self.initial_w, self.initial_h
                x2, y2 = x1 + w, y1 + h

                # Calculate and display the center of the bounding box
                center_x = (x1 + x2) // 2
                center_y = (y1 + y2) // 2
                self.center_listbox.insert(tk.END, f"(center_x = {center_x}, center_y = {center_y})")

                return x1, y1, x2, y2
        return None

    def update_bbox_rectangle(self, bbox):
        if bbox is not None:
            x1, y1, x2, y2 = map(int, bbox)
            if self.bbox_rect is not None:
                self.canvas.coords(self.bbox_rect, x1, y1, x2, y2)
                self.canvas.tag_raise(self.bbox_rect)  # Raise the bounding box to the front
            else:
                self.bbox_rect = self.canvas.create_rectangle(x1, y1, x2, y2, outline='#fc3d3d', width=8, tags="bbox")

    def show_frame(self):
        if self.video:
```

```python
            if not self.paused:
                if 0 <= self.frame_index < len(self.video):
                    if not self.frame_processing:  # Check if the frame is already being processed
                        try:
                            self.frame_processing = True  # Set frame_processing flag to True to indicate frame processing

                            frame = self.video.get_data(self.frame_index)
                            frame = cv2.cvtColor(frame, cv2.COLOR_RGB2BGR)

                            if self.bbox is not None:
                                if not self.tracking_started:
                                    self.tracking_started = True

                                self.bbox = self.track_object(frame, self.bbox)
                                if self.bbox:
                                    frame = cv2.cvtColor(frame, cv2.COLOR_BGR2RGB)
                                    frame = Image.fromarray(frame)
                                    frame = frame.resize((frame.width * self.zoom_scale.get(), frame.height * self.zoom_scale.get()))
                                    photo = ImageTk.PhotoImage(frame)
                                    self.photo = photo
                                    self.canvas.delete("video")
                                    self.canvas.create_image(0, 0, anchor="nw", image=photo, tags="video")

                                    self.update_bbox_rectangle(self.bbox)

                            else:
                                frame = cv2.cvtColor(frame, cv2.COLOR_BGR2RGB)
                                frame = Image.fromarray(frame)
                                frame = frame.resize((frame.width * self.zoom_scale.get(), frame.height * self.zoom_scale.get()))
                                photo = ImageTk.PhotoImage(frame)
                                self.photo = photo
                                self.canvas.delete("video")
                                self.canvas.create_image(0, 0, anchor="nw", image=photo, tags="video")

                            self.frame_number_label.config(text=f"Frame: {self.frame_index} / {self.video.count_frames()}", font=("Helvetica", 18))

                            self.frame_index += 1

                        except Exception as e:
                            print("Error: ", e)
                        finally:
```

```python
                            self.frame_processing = False  # Reset frame_processing
flag to False after processing the frame

    def on_mousewheel(self, event):
        direction = event.delta // 120
        current_value = int(self.zoom_scale.get())
        if direction == 1 and current_value < 10:
            current_value += 1
        elif direction == -1 and current_value > 1:
            current_value -= 1
        self.zoom_scale.set(current_value)
        self.update_zoom()

    def on_press(self, event):
        self.tracker = None
        self.start_x = self.canvas.canvasx(event.x)
        self.start_y = self.canvas.canvasy(event.y)
        # Clear the previous bounding box if it exists
        if self.bbox_rect:
            self.canvas.delete(self.bbox_rect)
            self.bbox_rect = None
        self.bbox = None
        self.bbox2 = None

    def on_drag(self, event):
        # Update the endpoint of the rectangle as the mouse moves
        cur_x = self.canvas.canvasx(event.x)
        cur_y = self.canvas.canvasy(event.y)

        # Define the coordinates correctly ensuring x1 < x2 and y1 < y2
        x1, y1 = min(self.start_x, cur_x), min(self.start_y, cur_y)
        x2, y2 = max(self.start_x, cur_x), max(self.start_y, cur_y)

        # Update dimensions for tracking
        self.initial_w = x2 - x1
        self.initial_h = y2 - y1
        self.bbox = (x1, y1, self.initial_w, self.initial_h)
        self.bbox2 = (self.start_x, self.start_y, cur_x, cur_y)

        # Update or create a rectangle on the canvas
        if self.bbox_rect:
            self.canvas.coords(self.bbox_rect, x1, y1, x2, y2)
        else:
            self.bbox_rect = self.canvas.create_rectangle(x1, y1, x2, y2,
outline="cyan", width=6)

    def prev_frame(self):
        if self.frame_index > 0:
```

```python
            self.frame_index -= 1
            self.show_frame()

    def next_frame(self):
        if self.video and self.frame_index < len(self.video) - 1:
            self.show_frame()

    def clear_listbox(self):
        self.center_listbox.delete(0, tk.END)

    def set_window_title(self):
        if self.file_name:
            self.master.title(f"Object Tracking with Boosting Tracker - {self.file_name}")
            self.master.title_font = ("Helvetica", 16, "bold")
        else:
            self.master.title("Object Tracking with Boosting Tracker")

    def on_release(self, self, event):
        self.analyze_histogram()  # Call analyze_histogram() method when the mouse button is released

    def analyze_histogram(self):
        if self.bbox2 is not None and self.video:
            x1, y1, x2, y2 = map(int, self.bbox2)
            if x1 != x2 and y1 != y2:
                try:
                    frame = self.video.get_data(self.frame_index)
                    # Ensure the bounding box is within the frame boundaries
                    h, w, _ = frame.shape
                    x1, x2 = max(0, min(x1, w)), max(0, min(x2, w))
                    y1, y2 = max(0, min(y1, h)), max(0, min(y2, h))

                    # Ensure x1 < x2 and y1 < y2
                    x1, x2 = sorted([x1, x2])
                    y1, y2 = sorted([y1, y2])

                    cropped_frame = frame[y1:y2, x1:x2]
                    if cropped_frame.size > 0:
                        cropped_frame = cv2.cvtColor(cropped_frame, cv2.COLOR_BGR2RGB)

                        # Get selected filter from combobox
                        selected_filter = self.filter_combobox.get()
                        # Apply selected filter
                        filtered_frame = self.apply_filter(selected_filter, cropped_frame)
```

```python
                    self.create_popup_window(filtered_frame)
                    self.display_cropped_image(filtered_frame)
                    self.display_histograms(filtered_frame)
                else:
                    print("Cropped frame is empty.")
            except Exception as e:
                print("Failed to process frame:", e)
        else:
            print("Bounding box dimensions are zero or negative.")

def create_popup_window(self, cropped_frame):
    self.popup_window = tk.Toplevel(self.master)
    self.popup_window.title("Cropped Image and Its Histogram")
    self.popup_window.geometry("1500x700")

def display_cropped_image(self, cropped_frame):
    cropped_frame_frame = tk.Frame(self.popup_window)
    cropped_frame_frame.pack(side="left")

    cropped_frame_rgb = cv2.cvtColor(cropped_frame, cv2.COLOR_BGR2RGB)
    cropped_img = Image.fromarray(cropped_frame_rgb)
    cropped_img = cropped_img.resize((600, 600))

    cropped_photo = ImageTk.PhotoImage(cropped_img)
    cropped_canvas = tk.Canvas(cropped_frame_frame, width=600, height=600)
    cropped_canvas.pack(side="left", anchor="nw")
    cropped_canvas.create_image(0, 0, anchor="nw", image=cropped_photo)
    cropped_canvas.image = cropped_photo

def display_histograms(self, cropped_frame):
    histograms_frame = tk.Frame(self.popup_window)
    histograms_frame.pack(side="right", padx=20)

    self.display_line_histogram(cropped_frame, histograms_frame)
    self.display_bar_histogram(cropped_frame, histograms_frame)

def display_line_histogram(self, cropped_frame, histograms_frame):
    line_histogram_frame = tk.Frame(histograms_frame)
    line_histogram_frame.pack(side="top", pady=10)

    plt.figure(figsize=(12, 4))
    color = ('r', 'g', 'b')
    for i, col in enumerate(color):
        histr = cv2.calcHist([cropped_frame], [i], None, [256], [0, 256])
        plt.plot(histr, color=col, label=f'Channel {col.upper()}', linewidth=2)
        plt.xlim([0, 256])
    plt.title('Line Histogram')
    plt.xlabel('Pixel Value')
```

```python
        plt.ylabel('Frequency')
        plt.tight_layout()
        plt.grid(True)
        plt.legend()

        line_histogram_img = self.plot_to_image(plt)
        self.display_histogram_image(line_histogram_frame, line_histogram_img)

    def display_bar_histogram(self, cropped_frame, histograms_frame):
        bar_histogram_frame = tk.Frame(histograms_frame)
        bar_histogram_frame.pack(side="bottom", pady=10)

        plt.figure(figsize=(12, 4))
        color = ('r', 'g', 'b')
        for i, col in enumerate(color):
            hist_range = (0, 256)
            hist_counts, _ = np.histogram(cropped_frame[:, :, i], bins=64, range=hist_range)
            plt.bar(np.arange(64), hist_counts, color=col, alpha=0.7, label=f'Channel {col.upper()}')
            for index, value in enumerate(hist_counts):
                plt.text(index, value + 10, str(int(value)), ha='center', va='bottom', fontsize=9)

        plt.title('Bar Histogram')
        plt.xlabel('Pixel Value')
        plt.ylabel('Frequency')
        plt.xticks(np.linspace(0, 63, num=5), np.linspace(0, 255, num=5, dtype=int))
        # Adjust x-axis ticks
        plt.tight_layout()
        plt.grid(True)
        plt.legend()

        bar_histogram_img = self.plot_to_image(plt)
        self.display_histogram_image(bar_histogram_frame, bar_histogram_img)

    def display_histogram_image(self, parent_frame, img):
        histogram_photo = ImageTk.PhotoImage(image=img)
        histogram_canvas = tk.Canvas(parent_frame, width=900, height=300)
        histogram_canvas.pack(side="bottom", anchor="se")
        histogram_canvas.create_image(0, 0, anchor="nw", image=histogram_photo)
        histogram_canvas.image = histogram_photo

    def plot_histogram_bar_to_image(self, image):
        # Calculate histogram for each channel
        histograms = []
        for i in range(3):
            hist_range = (0, 256)
```

```python
            hist_counts, _ = np.histogram(image[:, :, i], bins=64, range=hist_range)  
# Adjust bins to 64
            histograms.append(hist_counts)

        # Extracting only 64 bins from the histogram
        num_bins = 64  # Adjusted to 64 bins

        # Generating colors for each channel
        colors = ['red', 'green', 'blue']

        plt.figure()
        for i, histogram in enumerate(histograms):
            # Normalize the histogram counts for better visualization
            hist_counts = histogram / np.sum(histogram)
            # Setting the color for each channel
            plt.bar(np.arange(num_bins), hist_counts[:num_bins], color=colors[i],
alpha=0.7, label=f'Channel {["Red", "Green", "Blue"][i]}')

        plt.xlabel('Pixel Value')
        plt.ylabel('Normalized Frequency')
        plt.title('RGB Channel Histograms')
        plt.grid(True)
        plt.tight_layout()
        plt.legend()

        # Convert the histogram bar graph to an image
        histogram_bar_img = self.plot_to_image(plt)
        histogram_bar_photo = ImageTk.PhotoImage(image=histogram_bar_img)

        return histogram_bar_photo

    def plot_to_image(self, plt):
        plt.savefig('temp_plot.png')
        img = Image.open('temp_plot.png')
        return img

    def apply_filter(self, filter_name, frame):
        if filter_name == "None":
            return frame
        elif filter_name == "Gaussian":
            return cv2.GaussianBlur(frame, (5, 5), 0)
        elif filter_name == "Mean":
            return cv2.blur(frame, (5, 5))
        elif filter_name == "Median":
            return cv2.medianBlur(frame, 5)
        elif filter_name == "Bilateral Filtering":
            return cv2.bilateralFilter(frame, 9, 75, 75)
        elif filter_name == "Non-local Means Denoising":
```

```python
            return cv2.fastNlMeansDenoisingColored(frame, None, 10, 10, 7, 21)
        elif filter_name == "Anisotropic Diffusion":
            return self.anisotropic_diffusion(frame)
        elif filter_name == "Total Variation Denoising":
            return self.total_variation_denoising(frame)
        elif filter_name == "Wiener Filter":
            return self.wiener_filter(frame)
        elif filter_name == "Adaptive Thresholding":
            return self.adaptive_threshold_each_channel(frame)
        elif filter_name == "Haar Wavelet Transform":
            return self.haar_wavelet_transform(frame)
        elif filter_name == "Daubechies Wavelet Transform":
            return self.daubechies_wavelet_transform(frame)
        else:
            return frame  # Default: return original frame if filter not found

    def wiener_filter(self, frame, kernel_size=(5, 5), noise_var=0.01):
        # Check if frame is None
        if frame is None:
            print("Error: Input frame is None.")
            return None

        # Check if frame is a valid numpy array
        if not isinstance(frame, np.ndarray):
            print("Error: Input frame is not a numpy array.")
            return None

        # Check if frame is an empty array
        if frame.size == 0:
            print("Error: Input frame is empty.")
            return None

        # Check if frame is in BGR color space
        if frame.shape[-1] != 3:
            print("Error: Input frame is not in BGR color space.")
            return None

        # Apply Wiener filter
        filtered_frame = cv2.medianBlur(frame, kernel_size[0])  # Use kernel_size[0] as the kernel size
        filtered_frame = cv2.fastNlMeansDenoising(filtered_frame, h=noise_var)
        return filtered_frame

    def adaptive_threshold_each_channel(self, frame):
        # Split the frame into individual channels
        b, g, r = cv2.split(frame)

        # Apply adaptive thresholding to each channel separately
```

```python
        b_thresh = cv2.adaptiveThreshold(b, 255, cv2.ADAPTIVE_THRESH_GAUSSIAN_C,
cv2.THRESH_BINARY, 11, 2)
        g_thresh = cv2.adaptiveThreshold(g, 255, cv2.ADAPTIVE_THRESH_GAUSSIAN_C,
cv2.THRESH_BINARY, 11, 2)
        r_thresh = cv2.adaptiveThreshold(r, 255, cv2.ADAPTIVE_THRESH_GAUSSIAN_C,
cv2.THRESH_BINARY, 11, 2)

        # Merge the thresholded channels back together
        return cv2.merge([b_thresh, g_thresh, r_thresh])

    def haar_wavelet_transform(self, frame):
        # Split the frame into its individual color channels
        b, g, r = cv2.split(frame)

        # Perform the wavelet transform on each channel separately
        b_coeffs = pywt.dwt2(b, 'haar')
        g_coeffs = pywt.dwt2(g, 'haar')
        r_coeffs = pywt.dwt2(r, 'haar')

        # Reconstruct the channels from the coefficients
        b_reconstructed = pywt.idwt2(b_coeffs, 'haar')
        g_reconstructed = pywt.idwt2(g_coeffs, 'haar')
        r_reconstructed = pywt.idwt2(r_coeffs, 'haar')

        # Clip the values to ensure they are within the valid range
        b_reconstructed = np.clip(b_reconstructed, 0, 255).astype(np.uint8)
        g_reconstructed = np.clip(g_reconstructed, 0, 255).astype(np.uint8)
        r_reconstructed = np.clip(r_reconstructed, 0, 255).astype(np.uint8)

        # Merge the channels back together
        return cv2.merge([b_reconstructed, g_reconstructed, r_reconstructed])

    def daubechies_wavelet_transform(self, frame):
        # Split the frame into its individual color channels
        b, g, r = cv2.split(frame)

        # Choose the wavelet function (Daubechies 5)
        wavelet = 'db5'

        # Perform the wavelet transform on each channel separately
        b_coeffs = pywt.dwt2(b, wavelet)
        g_coeffs = pywt.dwt2(g, wavelet)
        r_coeffs = pywt.dwt2(r, wavelet)

        # Reconstruct the channels from the coefficients
        b_reconstructed = pywt.idwt2(b_coeffs, wavelet)
        g_reconstructed = pywt.idwt2(g_coeffs, wavelet)
        r_reconstructed = pywt.idwt2(r_coeffs, wavelet)
```

```python
        # Clip the values to ensure they are within the valid range
        b_reconstructed = np.clip(b_reconstructed, 0, 255).astype(np.uint8)
        g_reconstructed = np.clip(g_reconstructed, 0, 255).astype(np.uint8)
        r_reconstructed = np.clip(r_reconstructed, 0, 255).astype(np.uint8)

        # Merge the channels back together
        return cv2.merge([b_reconstructed, g_reconstructed, r_reconstructed])

    def anisotropic_diffusion(self, img):
        return cv2.fastNlMeansDenoisingColored(img, None, 10, 10, 7, 21)

    def apply_total_variation_denoising_channel(self, channel, weight, iterations):
        # Initialize the result with the original channel
        result = channel.copy().astype(np.float64)  # Convert to float64

        # Perform total variation denoising
        for _ in range(iterations):
            # Compute the gradient of the channel
            dx = cv2.Sobel(result, cv2.CV_64F, 1, 0, ksize=3)
            dy = cv2.Sobel(result, cv2.CV_64F, 0, 1, ksize=3)

            # Update the channel using the gradient and the weight
            result -= weight * np.sqrt(dx**2 + dy**2)

        # Clip the values to ensure they are within the valid range
        result = np.clip(result, 0, 255).astype(np.uint8)

        return result

    def total_variation_denoising(self, img, weight=0.01, iterations=20):
        # Split the image into its individual color channels
        b, g, r = cv2.split(img)

        # Apply total variation denoising to each channel separately
        b_denoised = self.apply_total_variation_denoising_channel(b, weight,
iterations)
        g_denoised = self.apply_total_variation_denoising_channel(g, weight,
iterations)
        r_denoised = self.apply_total_variation_denoising_channel(r, weight,
iterations)

        # Merge the denoised channels back together
        return cv2.merge([b_denoised, g_denoised, r_denoised])

def main():
    root = tk.Tk()
    app = BoostingTracker(root)
```

```
    root.mainloop()

if __name__ == "__main__":
    main()
```

OBJECT TRACKING WITH MEDIAN FLOW TRACKER

DESCRIPTION

The Python project MedianFlowTracker is a sophisticated application built using the Tkinter GUI library for Python, which allows users to track objects within video sequences using the MedianFlow tracking algorithm. The project integrates various aspects of digital image processing including object tracking, frame manipulation, and applying various filters to enhance video analysis capabilities.

Core Functionality

The core of the MedianFlowTracker application lies in its ability to open and play video files while dynamically tracking objects selected by the user. The main window of the application, initialized by Tkinter, hosts a variety of interactive elements such as buttons to control video playback (play, pause, stop), navigation through frames, and a zoom functionality to closely inspect details within frames. This is complemented by the ability to open video files and to start tracking at any point within these videos.

User Interaction

Upon loading a video, users can interact with the application by selecting an area of interest within the video frame using mouse inputs. This area is then used to initialize the MedianFlow tracker, a method well-suited for tracking objects with small and slow motion. The tracker operates by calculating the optical flow to predict the object's displacement and uses a median of these predictions to improve robustness against outliers, hence the name MedianFlow.

Advanced Settings and Customization

The application also features advanced settings that allow users to tailor the tracking process to their specific needs. Parameters such as window size, the number of points in the grid, maximum levels, and iterations can be adjusted. These settings fine-tune the tracker's behavior, making it adaptable to various types of video content and tracking requirements.

Visualization and Analysis Tools

To aid in analysis, MedianFlowTracker includes tools to visualize the tracking process. The application not only shows the current frame of the video but also draws a bounding box around the tracked object, updating it as the video plays. Additionally, it provides a list box that logs the center coordinates of the tracking box for each frame, useful for detailed analysis and debugging of the tracking process.

Filtering and Image Processing

A unique aspect of the application is its integration of various image processing filters that can be applied to video frames. These include Gaussian and median blurring, bilateral filtering, non-local means denoising, and more advanced techniques like anisotropic diffusion and wavelet transforms. Such filters can preprocess frames to enhance tracking accuracy or to simply explore different image processing techniques within an interactive environment.

Extension and Integration

Designed with extensibility in mind, the application architecture allows for the addition of more sophisticated image processing algorithms and tracking techniques. The clean separation between GUI controls and processing logic ensures that enhancements like adding new filters or integrating different tracking algorithms can be done with minimal changes to the existing codebase.

This project serves as a comprehensive tool for users interested in video analysis, offering both robust tracking capabilities and rich options for customization and extension. It is suitable for educational purposes, research in digital image processing, and practical applications requiring object tracking in video sequences.

CREATING WIDGETS

```python
def create_widgets(self):
    # Panel for video display
    video_panel = tk.Frame(self.master)
    video_panel.pack(padx=10, pady=10)

    # Canvas to display the original video
    canvas_width = 800
    canvas_height = 500
    self.canvas = tk.Canvas(video_panel, width=canvas_width, height=canvas_height)
    self.canvas.pack(side="left", fill="both", expand=True)
    self.canvas.bind("<MouseWheel>", self.on_mousewheel)
    self.canvas.bind("<ButtonPress-1>", self.on_press)
    self.canvas.bind("<B1-Motion>", self.on_drag)
    self.canvas.bind("<ButtonRelease-1>", self.on_release)  # Bind ButtonRelease event
```

```python
        # List box to display center coordinates
        self.center_listbox = tk.Listbox(video_panel, width=30, height=20, font=("Helvetica", 14))
        self.center_listbox.pack(side="right", fill="y")
        # Scrollbar for the listbox
        scrollbar = tk.Scrollbar(video_panel, orient="vertical")
        scrollbar.pack(side="left", fill="y")
        scrollbar.config(command=self.center_listbox.yview)

        # Attach scrollbar to listbox
        self.center_listbox.config(yscrollcommand=scrollbar.set)

        # Panel for control buttons
        control_panel = tk.Frame(self.master)
        control_panel.pack(padx=10, pady=(0, 10), fill="x")

        # Button to open a video file
        self.open_button = tk.Button(control_panel, text="Open Video", command=self.open_video)
        self.open_button.grid(row=0, column=0, padx=10, pady=5)

        # Combobox for selecting zoom scale
        self.zoom_combobox = ttk.Combobox(control_panel, textvariable=self.zoom_scale, values=list(range(1, 11)))
        self.zoom_combobox.grid(row=0, column=1, padx=10, pady=5)
        self.zoom_combobox.bind("<<ComboboxSelected>>", self.update_zoom)

        # Button to play/pause the video
        self.play_button = tk.Button(control_panel, text="Play/Pause", command=self.toggle_play_pause)
        self.play_button.grid(row=0, column=2, padx=10, pady=5)

        # Button to stop the video
        self.stop_button = tk.Button(control_panel, text="Stop", command=self.stop_video)
        self.stop_button.grid(row=0, column=3, padx=10, pady=5)

        # Button to navigate to the previous frame
        self.prev_frame_button = tk.Button(control_panel, text="Previous Frame", command=self.prev_frame)
        self.prev_frame_button.grid(row=0, column=4, padx=10, pady=5)

        # Button to navigate to the next frame
        self.next_frame_button = tk.Button(control_panel, text="Next Frame", command=self.next_frame)
        self.next_frame_button.grid(row=0, column=5, padx=10, pady=5)

        # Button to clear the listbox
```

```python
        self.clear_button = tk.Button(control_panel, text="Clear Listbox", 
            command=self.clear_listbox)
        self.clear_button.grid(row=0, column=6, padx=10, pady=5)

        # Label and entry for specifying scale
        self.scale_label = tk.Label(control_panel, text="Scale:")
        self.scale_label.grid(row=0, column=7, padx=10, pady=5, sticky="e")
        self.scale_default = tk.StringVar(value="1")
        self.scale_entry = ttk.Entry(control_panel, textvariable=self.scale_default)
        self.scale_entry.grid(row=0, column=8, padx=10, pady=5, sticky="w")
        self.scale_entry.bind("<Return>", lambda event: self.toggle_play_pause())

        # Combobox for selecting filters
        self.filter_combobox = ttk.Combobox(control_panel, values=self.filters)
        self.filter_combobox.grid(row=0, column=9, padx=10, pady=5)
        self.filter_combobox.current(0)  # Set default value

        # Label and entry for specifying Window Size
        self.win_label = tk.Label(control_panel, text="Window Size:")
        self.win_label.grid(row=1, column=0, padx=10, pady=5, sticky="e")
        self.win_default = tk.StringVar(value="15")
        self.win_entry = ttk.Entry(control_panel, textvariable=self.win_default)
        self.win_entry.grid(row=1, column=1, padx=10, pady=5, sticky="w")
        self.win_entry.bind("<Return>", lambda event: self.toggle_play_pause())

        # Label and entry for specifying max level
        self.level_label = tk.Label(control_panel, text="Max. Level:")
        self.level_label.grid(row=1, column=2, padx=10, pady=5, sticky="e")
        self.level_default = tk.StringVar(value="3")
        self.level_entry = ttk.Entry(control_panel, textvariable=self.level_default)
        self.level_entry.grid(row=1, column=3, padx=10, pady=5, sticky="w")
        self.level_entry.bind("<Return>", lambda event: self.toggle_play_pause())

        # Label and entry for specifying points in grid
        self.point_label = tk.Label(control_panel, text="Points In Grid:")
        self.point_label.grid(row=1, column=4, padx=10, pady=5, sticky="e")
        self.point_default = tk.StringVar(value="10")
        self.point_entry = ttk.Entry(control_panel, textvariable=self.point_default)
        self.point_entry.grid(row=1, column=5, padx=10, pady=5, sticky="w")
        self.point_entry.bind("<Return>", lambda event: self.toggle_play_pause())

        # Label and entry for specifying max iteration
        self.iter_label = tk.Label(control_panel, text="Max. Iteration:")
        self.iter_label.grid(row=1, column=6, padx=10, pady=5, sticky="e")
        self.iter_default = tk.StringVar(value="20")
        self.iter_entry = ttk.Entry(control_panel, textvariable=self.iter_default)
        self.iter_entry.grid(row=1, column=7, padx=10, pady=5, sticky="w")
        self.iter_entry.bind("<Return>", lambda event: self.toggle_play_pause())
```

```
        # Label and entry for specifying threshold
        self.thresh_label = tk.Label(control_panel, text="Epsilon:")
        self.thresh_label.grid(row=1, column=8, padx=10, pady=5, sticky="e")
        self.thresh_default = tk.StringVar(value="0.03")
        self.thresh_entry = ttk.Entry(control_panel, 
textvariable=self.thresh_default)
        self.thresh_entry.grid(row=1, column=9, padx=10, pady=5, sticky="w")
        self.thresh_entry.bind("<Return>", lambda event: self.toggle_play_pause())
```

The create_widgets()s method in the MedianFlowTracker application serves as a critical component in constructing the graphical user interface (GUI) and enabling user interaction. This method systematically sets up the various UI elements required for video tracking and processing tasks. Let's dissect the arrangement and functionality of each segment of this method.

Video Display Panel

- Video Panel: A frame (a container widget in Tkinter) is established to host the video display components. It's padded to ensure there's some space between its contents and the surrounding elements, enhancing visual clarity and user interaction.

- Canvas: The primary element within the video panel is the canvas, sized adequately to display video frames. This canvas will show the video's current frame and any superimposed graphical elements like bounding boxes for object tracking. The canvas binds several events to handle zooming with the mouse wheel and mouse actions for selecting objects to track.

Controls for Video Interaction

- Listbox and Scrollbar: These components are integrated for logging and displaying the center coordinates of the tracked object, crucial for analysis and debugging

purposes. The scrollbar enhances usability by allowing users to navigate through long lists of coordinates.
- Control Panel: This section hosts a series of buttons and input fields that control video playback, tracking parameters, and other settings. Here's a detailed breakdown:
- Basic Controls: Includes buttons to open a video file, play/pause the video, stop the video, and navigate through the video frame by frame. These controls are fundamental for any video analysis tool.
- Zoom Combobox: Allows users to select a zoom level for closer examination of the video, which is essential for precise tracking or when analyzing small or detailed objects.

Advanced Tracking Parameters
- Parameter Inputs: Several entry fields and labels are added to adjust tracking parameters dynamically. These include:
- Window Size, Max Level, Points in Grid: These settings directly influence the MedianFlow algorithm's performance and accuracy, offering users the flexibility to optimize tracking based on specific video characteristics or object behaviors.
- Maximum Iterations and Epsilon: These parameters control the termination criteria of the tracking process, where max iterations limit the number of iterations for the algorithm, and epsilon sets the threshold for stopping the iterations based on changes between steps.

Filter Selection
- Filter Combobox: A dropdown menu allows the selection of various image processing filters that can be applied to video frames. This feature is particularly

valuable for preprocessing frames to improve tracking accuracy or to explore image enhancements and effects.

Functionality and Interactivity

- Binding Actions: Key elements like the entry fields for parameters and the filter combobox are bound with events that trigger actions (toggle_play_pause) upon user interaction (e.g., pressing 'Return'). This setup ensures that parameter changes are applied immediately and efficiently without requiring additional buttons or commands.

Conclusion

The create_widgets() method efficiently organizes the GUI components into a user-friendly and functional layout. It not only facilitates essential video tracking tasks but also extends capabilities through interactive controls and customizable parameters, making it a robust tool for users needing detailed and dynamic video analysis. This method exemplifies thoughtful UI design by balancing between functionality and ease of use, enabling both novice and advanced users to engage effectively with the tool's features.

INIITALIZING TRACKER

```python
def initialize_tracker(self, frame, bbox, params=None):
    """Initialize the MedianFlow tracker with possible user-defined parameters."""

    # Default parameters for MedianFlow Tracker
    default_params = {
        'winSize': (int(self.win_entry.get()), int(self.win_entry.get())),
        'maxLevel': int(self.level_entry.get()),
        'pointsInGrid': int(self.point_entry.get()),
```

```python
            'termCriteria': (cv2.TERM_CRITERIA_COUNT + cv2.TERM_CRITERIA_EPS, 
int(self.iter_entry.get()), float(self.thresh_entry.get()))
        }

        # If params are provided, update the default_params
        if params:
            default_params.update(params)

        # Adjust bbox based on parameters such as scaling
        scale = int(self.scale_entry.get())  #scale is provided through a GUI element
        bbox = (
            int(bbox[0] + (1 - scale) * bbox[2] / 2),  # Center the scaling on the bbox
            int(bbox[1] + (1 - scale) * bbox[3] / 2),
            int(bbox[2] * scale),
            int(bbox[3] * scale)
        )

        # Initialize the Median Flow tracker
        self.tracker = cv2.legacy.TrackerMedianFlow_create()

        # Assuming a hypothetical method to set parameters (not available in the current OpenCV API)
        # This part is pseudo-code and will not work with standard OpenCV installations
        if hasattr(self.tracker, 'setParams'):
            self.tracker.setParams(default_params)

        self.tracker.init(frame, tuple(map(int, bbox)))
        self.initial_w, self.initial_h = bbox[2], bbox[3]
```

The initialize_tracker() method is designed to configure and initiate the tracking process for a selected object within a video frame. This method is essential for setting up the MedianFlow tracker with specific parameters that can be adjusted according to user preferences or specific tracking requirements. Here's a detailed breakdown of each part of the method:

Setting up Default Parameters
- Default Parameters: The method begins by establishing a dictionary of default parameters necessary for the MedianFlow tracker. These parameters include:

- winSize: The size of the search window at each pyramid level, crucial for the accuracy and performance of the tracker.
- maxLevel: The 0-based maximal pyramid level number; if set to 0, pyramids are not used (single level), if set to 1, two levels are used, and so on.
- pointsInGrid: The number of points in the grid used in the tracking algorithm, affecting the granularity of the search.
- termCriteria: Criteria for terminating the tracking process, which could be based on the count of iterations and/or the change in parameters between iterations, ensuring precision and preventing endless loops.

Customization Through Parameters

- Parameter Customization: If additional parameters are passed to the method, these are merged with the default parameters. This allows for dynamic adjustments based on runtime decisions or user inputs, enhancing flexibility and adaptability of the tracking.
- Adjusting the Bounding Box
  - Scaling the Bounding Box: The bounding box (bbox) coordinates are adjusted based on a scaling parameter obtained from the user interface. This adjustment ensures that the tracker focuses on a scaled area of the initial selection, which can be crucial for focusing on the most relevant features of the object, especially in cases where the initial bounding box might need refinement or resizing.

Tracker Initialization

Tracker Creation: An instance of the MedianFlow tracker is created using OpenCV's legacy API. This step is crucial as it prepares the tracker with the foundational algorithm required to follow the object through the video frames.

- Parameter Setting (Pseudo-Code): The method includes a hypothetical check to set additional parameters directly to the tracker. This part is noted as pseudo-code because current OpenCV API versions do not directly support setting parameters in this way for the MedianFlow tracker.
- Tracker Initialization: The tracker is then initialized with the frame and the adjusted bounding box. This step effectively starts the tracking process, using the frame as the base and the bbox to specify the object's location.

Record Initial Dimensions

- Recording Dimensions: After initializing the tracker, the method records the width and height of the bounding box. These values are essential for maintaining a consistent tracking window size across the video, which helps in accurately evaluating the movement and changes in the appearance of the tracked object.

Method Summary

This method encapsulates the initialization of the tracking process, setting a solid foundation for the MedianFlow tracker to function correctly throughout the video. By allowing parameter customization and adjusting the tracking window according to user inputs, it provides a robust and flexible approach to object tracking in video sequences. This setup is crucial for applications requiring precision and adaptability, such as in surveillance, sports analysis, or any interactive media where tracking movement is vital.

TRACKING OBJECT

```python
def track_object(self, frame, bbox, user_params=None):
    """Track object using MedianFlow Tracker with optional user parameters."""
    if bbox:
        if self.tracker is None:
            self.initialize_tracker(frame, bbox, user_params)

        # Update the tracker and get the new bounding box
        success, bbox = self.tracker.update(frame)
        if success:
            x1, y1, w, h = map(int, bbox)
            # Use the dimensions as tracked, no adjustment to maintain initial dimensions
            x2, y2 = x1 + w, y1 + h

            # Calculate and display the center of the bounding box
            center_x = (x1 + x2) // 2
            center_y = (y1 + y2) // 2
            self.center_listbox.insert(tk.END, f"(center_x = {center_x}, center_y = {center_y})")

            return x1, y1, x2, y2
    return None
```

The track_object() method in MedianFlowTracker application plays a pivotal role in the ongoing tracking process throughout the video sequence. Here's a detailed explanation of how this method operates and effectively tracks an object within a video frame using the MedianFlow tracking algorithm integrated via OpenCV:

Functionality Overview

This method is designed to continuously track an object within a video after its initial detection and bounding box setup. The tracking is based on the object's position in one frame to predict its position in subsequent frames, using the MedianFlow algorithm, which is particularly effective for objects with small and predictable motion.

Step-by-Step Breakdown
1. Check Bounding Box Availability:
    - Purpose: Ensures that there is an initial bounding box (bbox) provided. If not, the method returns None, indicating no tracking process can be initiated or continued.
    - Process: The method starts by verifying if a bbox exists. This bounding box defines the region of interest where the object was detected or defined by the user.
2. Tracker Initialization:
    - Condition: If the tracker instance is None, it suggests that the tracker has not been initialized yet.
    - Initialization: Calls the initialize_tracker method with the current frame, the bounding box, and any user-defined parameters. This step sets up the MedianFlow tracker with the necessary configurations tailored to the specifics of the current tracking task.
3. Update Tracker:
    - Tracking Update: Uses the update method of the MedianFlow tracker to determine the new position of the object in the current frame based on its previous state.
    - Success Check: The update method returns a tuple: a success flag and the new bounding box. If success is True, it indicates that the tracker has successfully located the object in the current frame.
    - New Bounding Box: Updates the bbox variable with the new coordinates of the tracked object.
4. Calculate and Display Center Coordinates:
    - Coordinate Calculation: Computes the center of the bounding box by averaging the coordinates. This gives a single point (center_x, center_y) that represents the central position of the object.

- Display in List Box: Inserts the center coordinates into the center_listbox, which logs these values for each frame, providing a useful trail of the object's movement through the video.
5. Return New Bounding Box Coordinates:
    - Coordinate Mapping: Translates the top-left and bottom-right corners of the bounding box from the tracking output to a format suitable for further processing or visualization.
    - Return Values: Returns a tuple consisting of the x and y coordinates of these corners, which can be used to draw the bounding box on the video or for further analysis.

Summary

The track_object() method is a core component of the object tracking functionality within the MedianFlowTracker application. It seamlessly integrates initialization, updating, and display of tracking results, making it a robust tool for real-time video analysis. This method's effectiveness in handling object tracking helps in applications such as surveillance, activity monitoring, or any interactive media where understanding object movement is crucial. By providing real-time updates and visual feedback, it enhances user interaction and allows for immediate assessment of the tracking performance.

RUNNING PROGRAM

Run program and choose certain frame by pushing Next Frame button. Then, draw a bounding box rectangle on certain object in the frame and push Next Frame button.

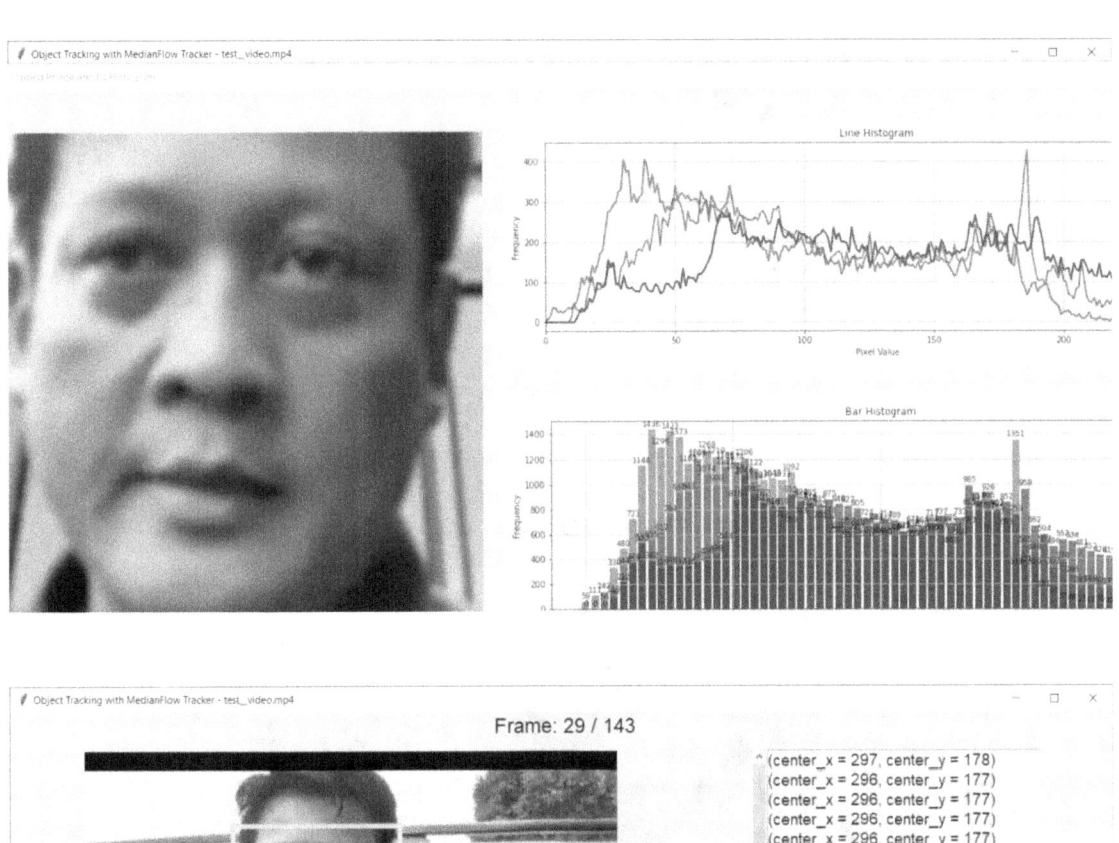

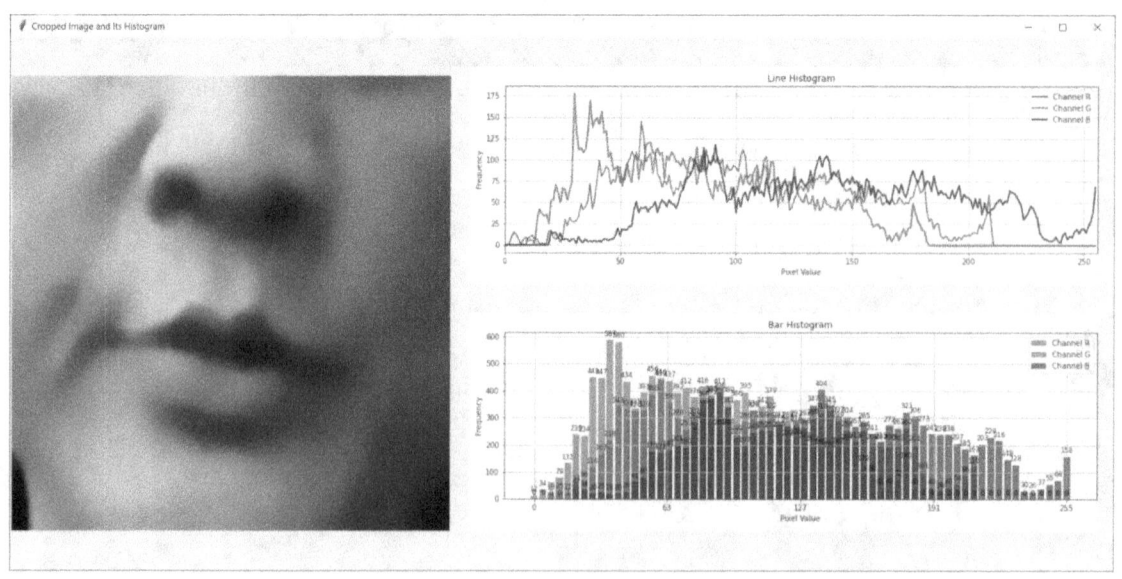

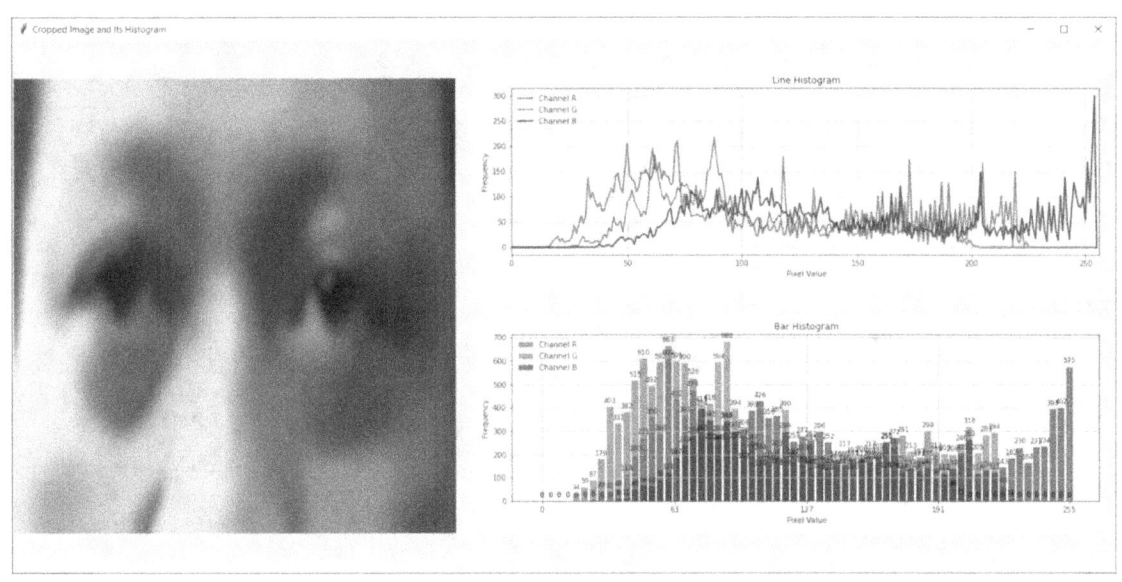

OBJECT TRACKING WITH MIL (MULTIPLE INSTANCE LEARNING) TRACKER

DESCRIPTION

The MILTracker project encapsulates a sophisticated application built using Python's Tkinter GUI library to implement object tracking through video sequences using the Multiple Instance Learning (MIL) tracking algorithm. This robust application allows users to interactively select and track objects within a video, leveraging advanced image processing techniques.

At the heart of the application is the MIL algorithm, a form of machine learning that is particularly effective for scenarios where there is ambiguity in labeling training instances. In the context of this tracker, the algorithm treats groups of pixels as "bags" where at least one instance in the bag is positive, making it well-suited for tracking through occlusions or other visual obfuscations that might occur in video feeds. This approach is integrated within the application to allow real-time tracking of objects as a video plays, with functionalities to adjust tracking parameters dynamically based on user input.

The GUI of the MILTracker is both intuitive and functional, featuring controls for loading and playing videos, adjusting zoom, and stepping through the video frame by frame. A key feature is the ability to manually select the object to be tracked by drawing a bounding box with the mouse. This input initializes the tracking process, with the application displaying the path of the object as the video continues to play. The interface also includes options to apply various image filters like Gaussian blurring or Median filtering, which can help in improving tracking accuracy by reducing noise or enhancing features.

Additional controls and settings allow users to fine-tune the tracking process. Parameters such as the size of the tracking window, the number of points in the grid for the MIL algorithm, and other advanced settings can be adjusted through dedicated input fields in the control panel. This level of customization ensures that the tracker can be adapted to different types of video content and tracking requirements.

For analysis and debugging, the application provides a log of the center coordinates of the tracking box for each frame, displayed in a list box. This feature is invaluable for those who need to record the trajectory or analyze the movement patterns of the tracked object. Moreover, the application is designed with extensibility in mind, allowing for the addition of new filters or tracking algorithms without significant overhauls to the existing codebase.

Overall, the MILTracker offers a powerful toolset for users ranging from hobbyists to professionals in fields such as surveillance, sports analysis, and any other domain requiring reliable object tracking. It demonstrates a practical application of machine learning algorithms in real-world scenarios, enhancing the capabilities of video analysis software.

TRACKING OBJECT

```python
    def initialize_tracker(self, frame, bbox, params=None):
        """Initialize the tracker with possible user-defined parameters."""
        if params:
            # Adjust bbox based on parameters such as scaling
            scale = int(self.scale_entry.get())  #scale is provided through a GUI element
            bbox = (
                bbox[0], bbox[1],
                int(bbox[2] * scale), int(bbox[3] * scale)
            )

        # Initialize the MIL tracker instead of Boosting
        self.tracker = cv2.legacy.TrackerMIL_create()  # Using legacy API as per the original setup
        self.tracker.init(frame, tuple(map(int, bbox)))
        self.initial_w, self.initial_h = bbox[2], bbox[3]

    def track_object(self, frame, bbox, user_params=None):
        """Track object using MIL Tracker with optional user parameters."""
        if bbox:
            if self.tracker is None:
                self.initialize_tracker(frame, bbox, user_params)

            # Update the tracker and get the new bounding box
            success, bbox = self.tracker.update(frame)
            if success:
                x1, y1, w, h = map(int, bbox)
                # Use stored initial dimensions (if this logic is required, otherwise adjust as needed)
                w, h = self.initial_w, self.initial_h
                x2, y2 = x1 + w, y1 + h

                # Calculate and display the center of the bounding box
                center_x = (x1 + x2) // 2
                center_y = (y1 + y2) // 2
                self.center_listbox.insert(tk.END, f"(center_x = {center_x}, center_y = {center_y})")

                return x1, y1, x2, y2
        return None
```

The methods initialize_tracker() and track_object() in MILTracker application are critical for setting up and maintaining object tracking using the Multiple Instance Learning (MIL) algorithm within a video sequence. Here's a detailed breakdown of both methods:

initialize_tracker() Method:

This method sets up the MIL tracker with the initial conditions necessary for tracking to commence.

- Parameter Handling:
  - Scaling: Before initializing the tracker, the method optionally adjusts the bounding box (bbox) dimensions based on a scaling factor provided by the user. This is particularly useful when the initial guess of the object's size needs refinement.
- Tracker Initialization:
  - Tracker Creation: An instance of the MIL tracker is created using OpenCV's legacy API, which supports various tracking algorithms including MIL.
  - Tracker Start: The tracker is then initialized with the first frame and the (possibly scaled) bounding box. This bbox specifies the region in the frame where the object of interest is located, serving as the starting point for the tracking process.
- Storing Initial Dimensions:
  - Dimension Storage: The method stores the initial dimensions of the bounding box. This information can be used later to maintain a consistent tracking window size or for adjustments during the tracking process.

track_object() Method:

This method handles the ongoing tracking of an object as new video frames are processed.

- Pre-Tracking Checks:

    Tracker Check: The method first checks if the tracker has been initialized. If not, it calls initialize_tracker to set up the tracker with the current frame and bounding box.

- Tracking Update:
    - Frame Update: The tracker's update method is called with the current video frame to locate the object. This method returns a success flag and an updated bounding box.
    - Success Check: If tracking is successful, the new bounding box is used to calculate the object's current position.

- Coordinate Calculation:

    Center Calculation: The method calculates the center of the bounding box. This central point is a simple way to represent the object's position in the frame and is logged in a list box for easy monitoring.

- Return New Coordinates:

    Output: The method returns the top-left and bottom-right coordinates of the updated bounding box. This can be used to draw the bounding box on the frame for visualization or for further analysis.

Conclusion:

Together, these methods enable the MILTracker application to robustly track objects across frames, adjusting dynamically to changes in object appearance and motion. This functionality is crucial for applications where accurate real-time tracking of objects is needed, such as in surveillance systems, sports analytics, or any interactive multimedia system. The ability to customize the tracking process through user-defined parameters and to visually monitor the tracking progress enhances the application's utility and user-friendliness.

RUNNING PROGRAM

Run program and choose certain frame by pushing Next Frame button. Then, draw a bounding box rectangle on certain object in the frame and push Next Frame button.

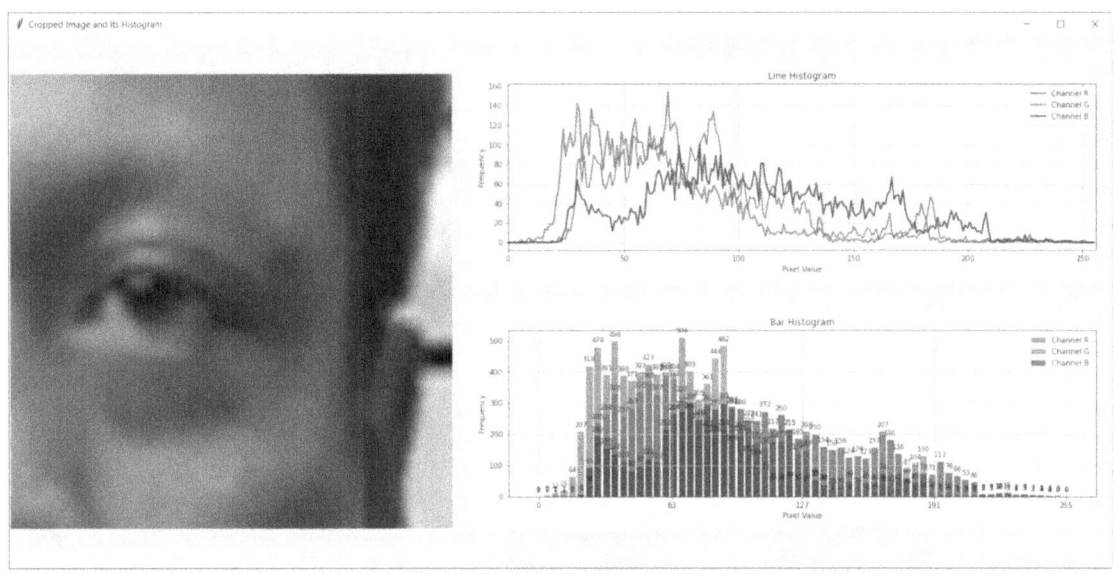

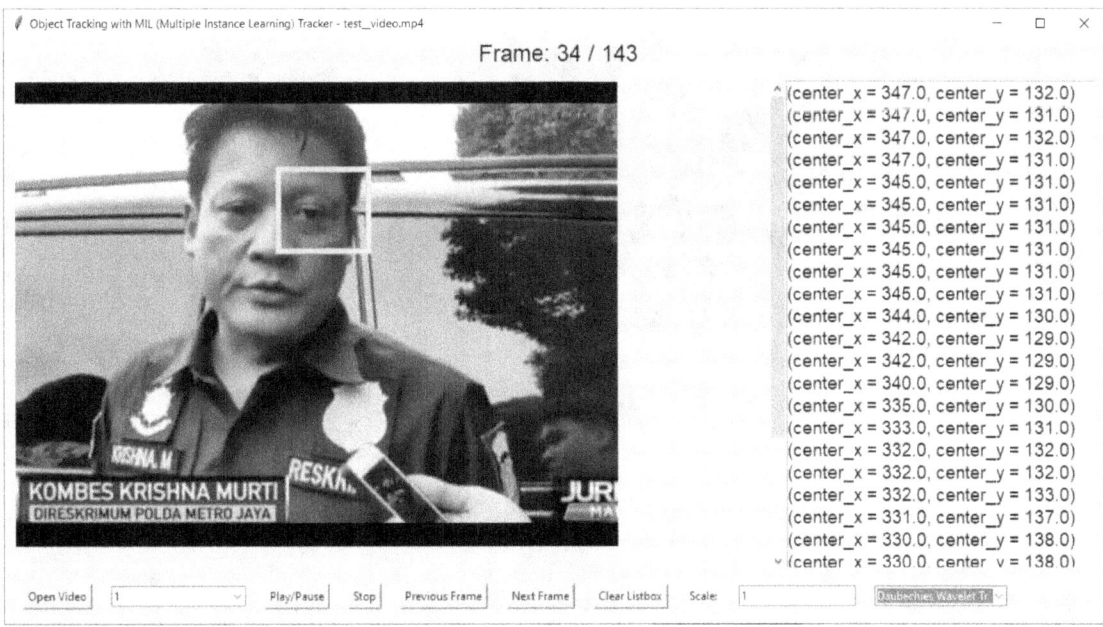

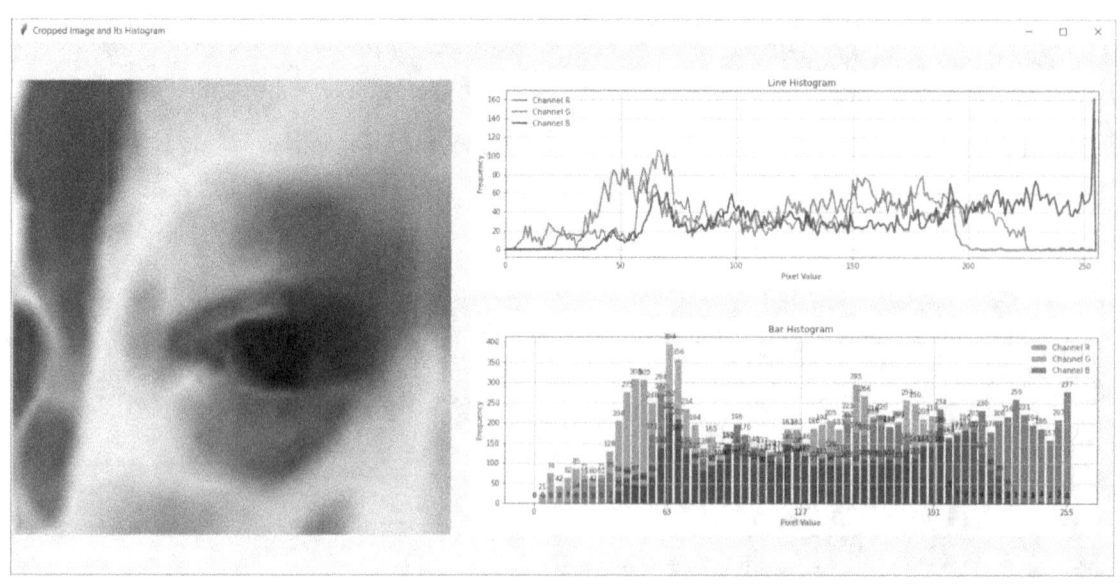

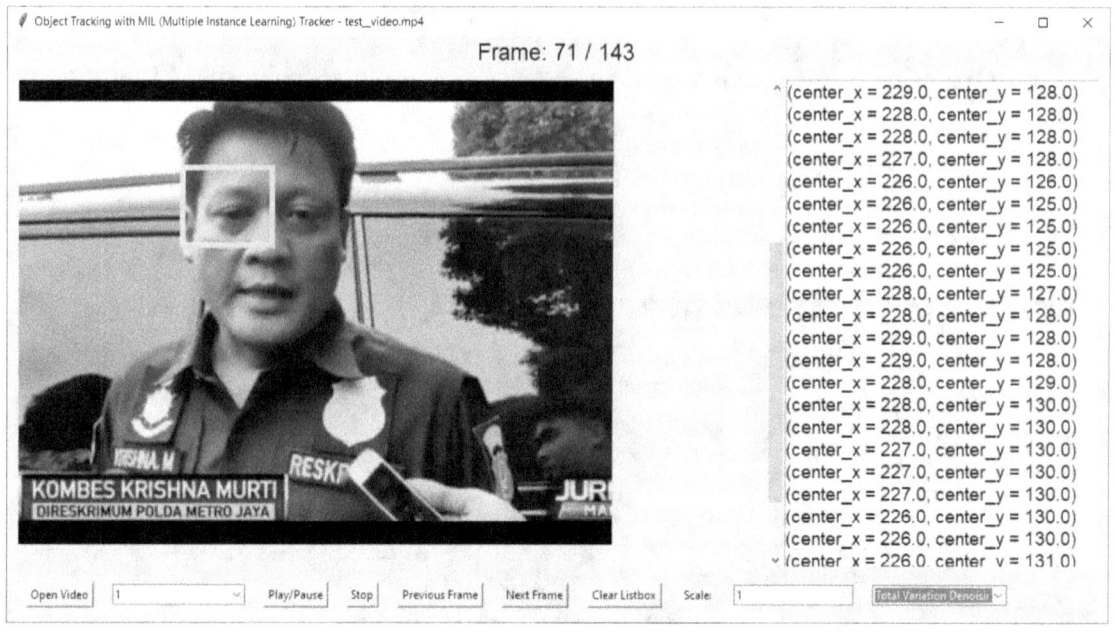

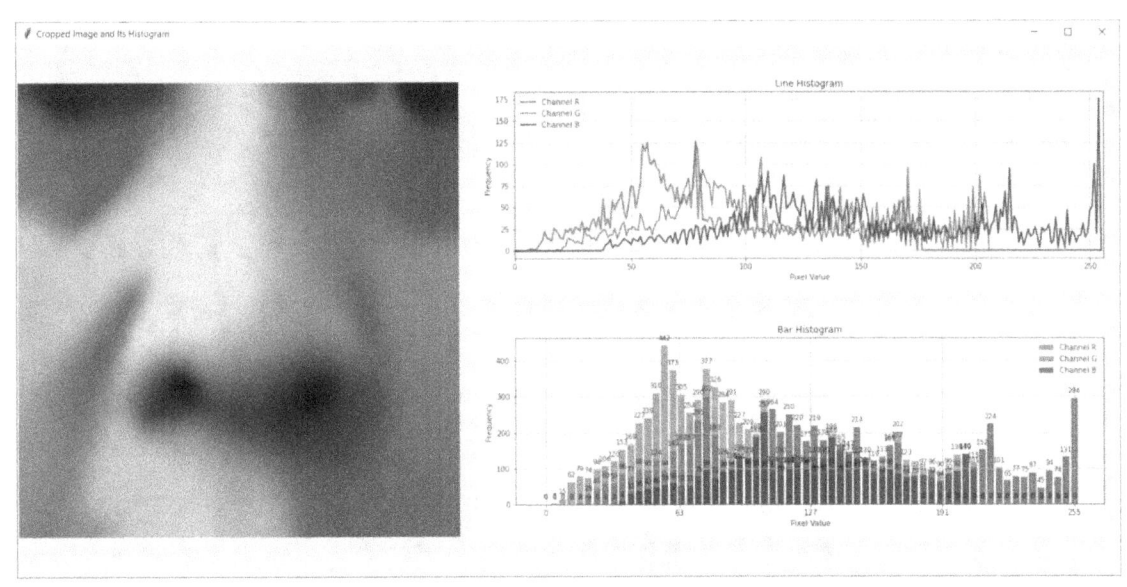

OBJECT TRACKING WITH MOSSE (MINIMUM OUTPUT SUM OF SQUARED ERROR) TRACKER

DESCRIPTION

The MOSSETracker project utilizes the MOSSE (Minimum Output Sum of Squared Error) tracking algorithm integrated into a GUI application developed with Python and the tkinter library. The application's interface is designed for simplicity and functionality, allowing users to load video files, control playback, and observe the tracking of objects in real time. The project integrates powerful OpenCV functions for video processing and object tracking, making it accessible and usable for individuals interested in computer vision applications.

Upon launching the application, users are presented with a straightforward layout comprising video playback controls, options for adjusting the zoom level of the video, and a list box displaying the coordinates of the tracked object's center. The interface also features a selection of image processing filters which can be applied to the video frames to potentially enhance tracking performance or for educational demonstrations of various image processing techniques. These filters include Gaussian blurring, median filtering, and more advanced methods like anisotropic diffusion and wavelet transformations.

The core functionality revolves around the MOSSE tracking algorithm, known for its efficiency and effectiveness in tracking objects in videos. Once a user loads a video and selects an initial bounding box around the object of interest, the MOSSE tracker is initialized with this information and begins tracking the object across the video frames. The application dynamically updates the display to show the current frame with the bounding box overlay, providing visual feedback on the tracker's performance.

Additional features of the application include the ability to manually adjust the bounding box by clicking and dragging over the video, which can be useful for correcting the tracker or reinitializing it mid-video. There is also functionality to analyze the histograms of selected video frame regions, allowing users to explore the color characteristics of objects within the bounding box. This can be particularly useful for educational purposes or in applications where color data is relevant.

In essence, the MOSSETracker project serves as a practical tool for demonstrating object tracking technology while providing a platform for further development and experimentation. Whether for educational purposes, research, or practical applications, this tracker offers a robust foundation for exploring video analysis and object tracking technologies within a user-friendly graphical interface.

TRACKING OBJECT

```python
    def initialize_tracker(self, frame, bbox, params=None):
        """Initialize the MOSSE tracker with possible user-defined parameters."""
        
        # Read scale factor from a GUI entry; ensure it is a float
        scale = float(self.scale_entry.get())
        
        # Adjust bbox based on the scaling parameter
        bbox = (
            int(bbox[0] + (1 - scale) * bbox[2] / 2),  # Center the scaling on the bbox
            int(bbox[1] + (1 - scale) * bbox[3] / 2),
            int(bbox[2] * scale),
            int(bbox[3] * scale)
        )
        
        # Initialize the MOSSE tracker
        self.tracker = cv2.legacy.TrackerMOSSE_create()
        
        # Initialize the tracker with the frame and adjusted bbox
        success = self.tracker.init(frame, tuple(map(int, bbox)))
        if not success:
            print("Tracker initialization failed.")
            return False
        
        self.initial_w, self.initial_h = bbox[2], bbox[3]
        return True
    
    def track_object(self, frame, bbox, user_params=None):
        """Track object using MOSSE Tracker with optional user parameters."""
        if not self.tracker:
            if not self.initialize_tracker(frame, bbox, user_params):
                return None
        
        # Update the tracker and get the new bounding box
        success, bbox = self.tracker.update(frame)
        if success:
            x1, y1, w, h = map(int, bbox)
            x2, y2 = x1 + w, y1 + h
            
            # Calculate and display the center of the bounding box
            center_x = (x1 + x2) // 2
            center_y = (y1 + y2) // 2
            if hasattr(self, 'center_listbox'):
```

```
            self.center_listbox.insert(tk.END, f"(center_x = {center_x}, center_y
= {center_y})")

        return (x1, y1, x2, y2)
    return None
```

The function initialize_tracker() in the MOSSETracker project is designed to set up the MOSSE (Minimum Output Sum of Squared Error) tracker with a specified bounding box and scale parameters derived from user input. This function begins by extracting a scaling factor from the graphical user interface, which the user can adjust to modify the size of the bounding box dynamically. This scale is applied symmetrically to the initial bounding box dimensions, effectively resizing the box to either focus on a smaller area or encompass a larger region around the object of interest.

Within the function, the adjusted bounding box coordinates are calculated by applying the scaling factor. The process involves recalculating each dimension of the bounding box based on the scale while ensuring the object remains centered within the adjusted box. After defining the new bounding box, the function initializes the MOSSE tracker using OpenCV's legacy API, passing the current video frame and the new bounding box as parameters.

The tracker's initialization is crucial as it sets up the internal state of the MOSSE tracker, allowing it to start tracking the object from the given position and size. If the initialization is successful, the function stores the dimensions of the bounding box, which can be used later for various purposes, such as adjusting the box during tracking or for re-initialization. In case the initialization fails, an error message is printed, and the function returns False indicating failure to initialize properly.

The track_object() function is designed to update the position of the bounding box using the MOSSE tracker as the video frames are processed. If the tracker is not already initialized, it will call the initialize_tracker function. Upon successful updating, this function retrieves the new bounding box coordinates, which indicate the current position of the tracked object. It calculates the center of this box, updating the user interface to show where the object is centered on the screen, thereby providing real-time feedback to the user.

This function is an integral part of the object tracking process in the application, allowing continuous monitoring and positional updates of the object being tracked. It handles the actual computation where the tracker predicts the new location of the object based on the visual data from subsequent video frames. If the tracker fails to update (i.e., loses track of the object), the function returns None, signaling an issue with tracking continuity. These two functions together enable robust tracking capabilities in the MOSSETracker application, facilitating educational demonstrations and practical usage in various tracking scenarios.

RUNNING PROGRAM

Run program and choose certain frame by pushing Next Frame button. Then, draw a bounding box rectangle on certain object in the frame and push Next Frame button.

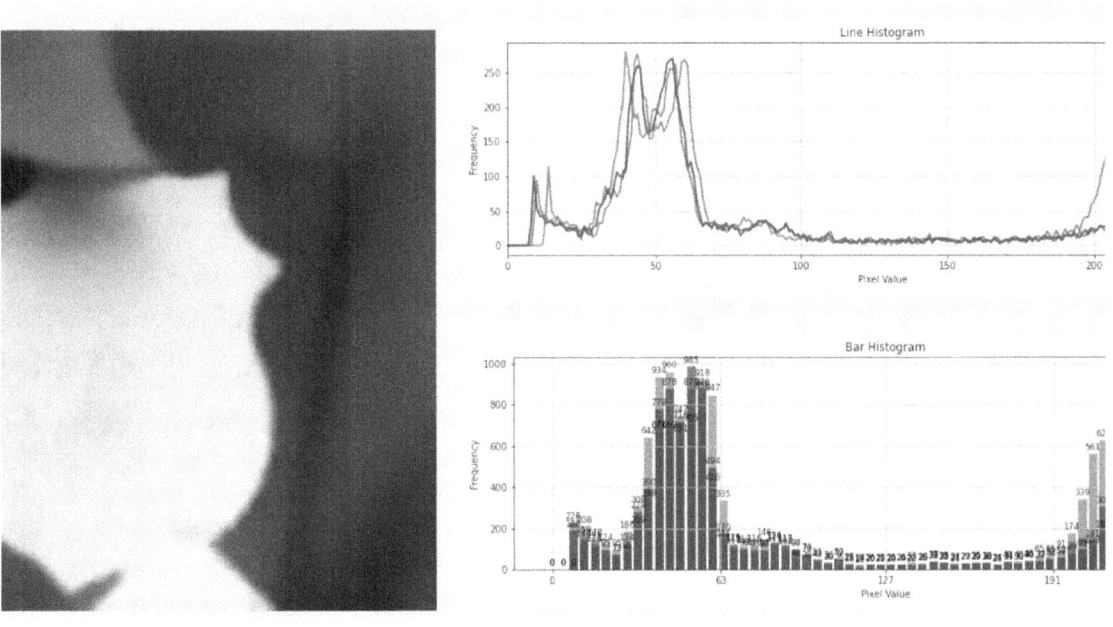

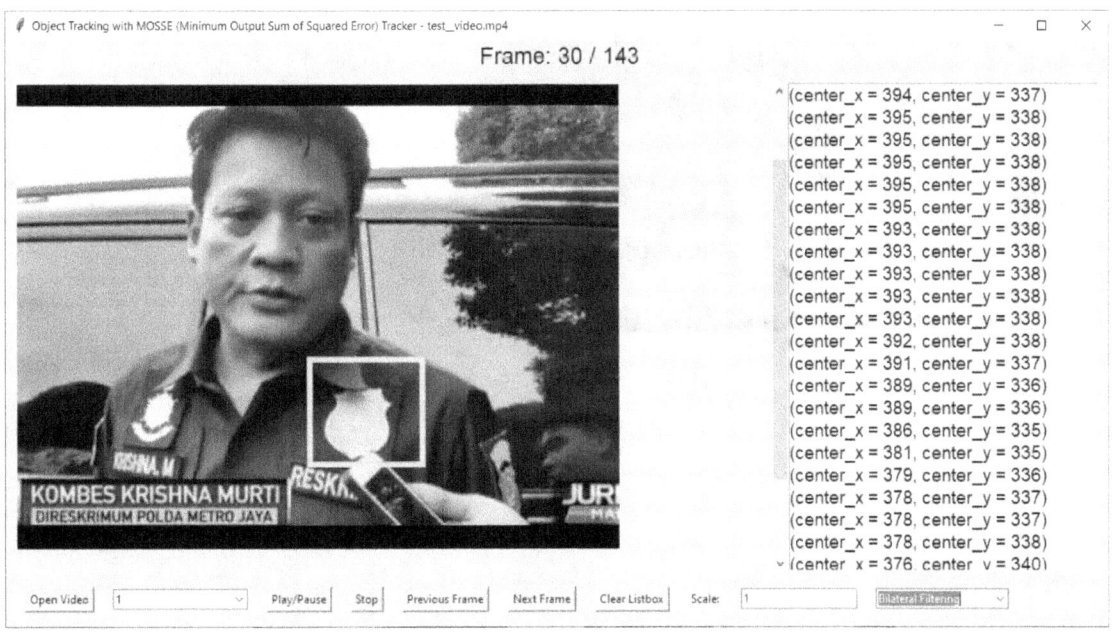

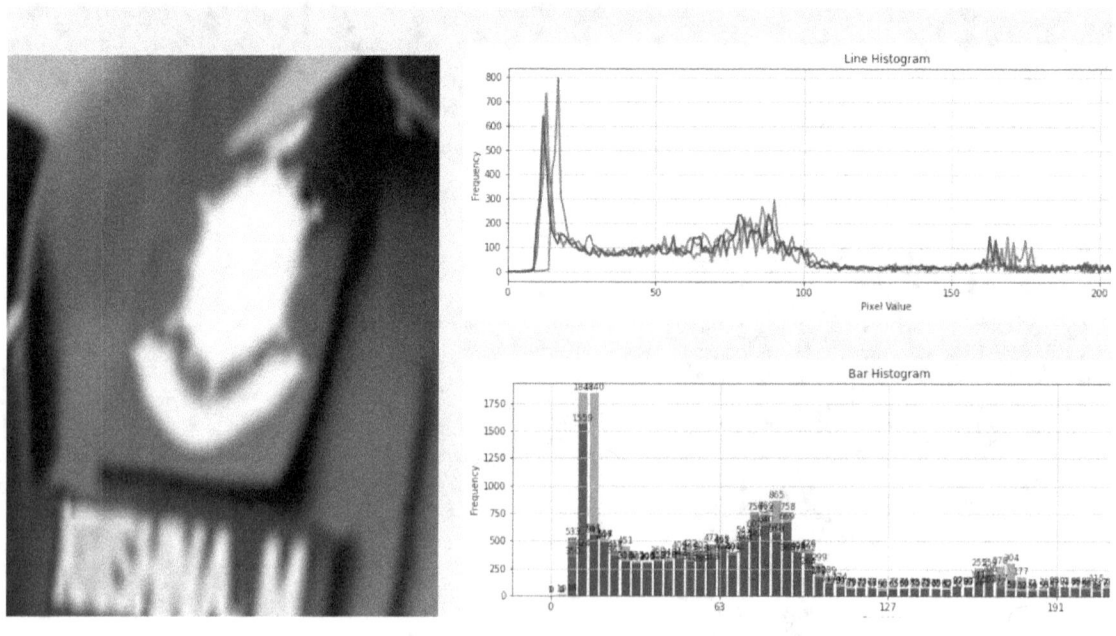

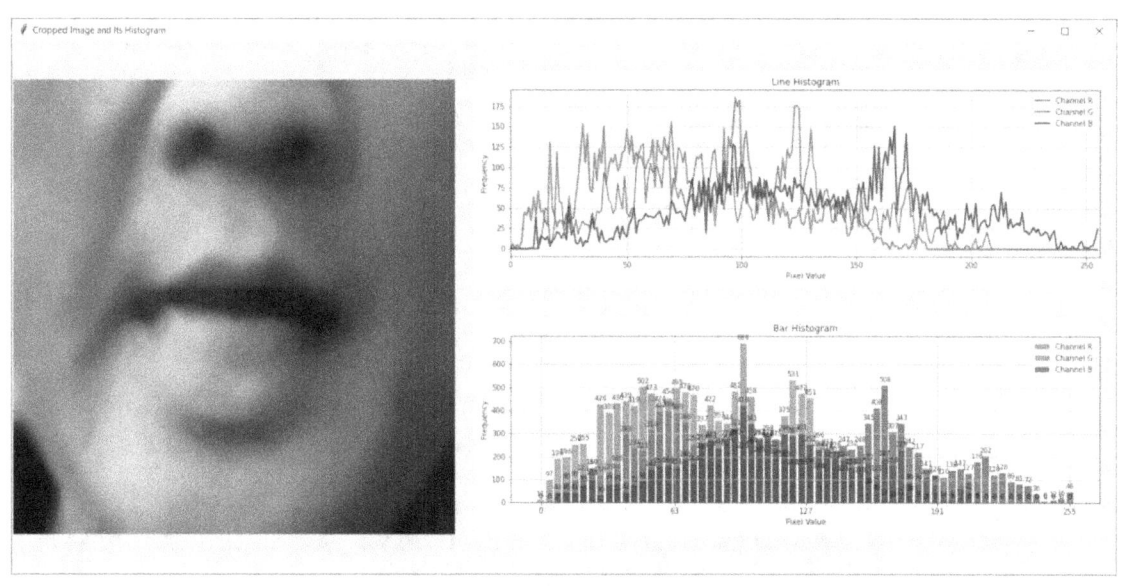

OBJECT TRACKING WITH MOSSE KCF (KERNELIZED CORRELATION FILTERS) TRACKER

DESCRIPTION

The project revolves around the KCFTracker application. This sophisticated application is built using Python, employing several libraries including Tkinter for GUI development, OpenCV for image processing, and ImageIO for handling video streams.

At the core of the application is a GUI framework that enables users to interact with video files for object tracking purposes. The GUI consists of various elements such as video display panels, control buttons, and adjustable settings for zoom, filter application, and tracker parameters. Users can load videos, control playback, select regions of interest by drawing bounding boxes, and observe the tracker's performance in real time. The tracker's bounding box, once set, can be adjusted and resized based on user input to ensure the focus remains on the object of interest throughout the tracking process.

A significant feature of this application is its ability to apply various image filters. These filters range from simple blurring and median filtering to more complex ones like bilateral filtering and wavelet transformations. Users can select these filters from a dropdown menu to enhance the video feed, which can be particularly useful in improving the tracker's accuracy under different visual conditions. This functionality is crucial for practical applications where lighting conditions and object textures might vary significantly.

The tracker initialization and object tracking functions are central to the application's operation. These functions handle the configuration of the tracker based on user-defined parameters, such as detection thresholds and scaling factors, which can be fine-tuned to optimize tracking performance. The actual tracking is conducted frame-by-frame as the video plays, with the tracker updating the position of the bounding box based on the movements of the target object within the video frame.

In addition to tracking, the application offers analytical tools such as histogram analysis, allowing users to examine the color distribution within selected areas of the video frame. This feature is accessible through a popup window that displays both the cropped image and its color histograms, providing insights into the image data that could be beneficial for further analysis or debugging tracker behavior. This holistic approach combining interactive controls, real-time processing, and analytical tools makes the KCFTracker a comprehensive tool for educational and development purposes in computer vision.

TRACKING OBJECT

```python
    def initialize_tracker(self, frame, bbox, params=None):
        """Initialize the KCF tracker with possible user-defined parameters."""

        # Default parameters for KCF Tracker
        default_params = {
            "detect_thresh": float(self.thresh_entry.get()),
            "sigma": float(self.sigma_entry.get()),
            "lambda": float(self.lambda_entry.get()),
            "interp_factor": float(self.factor_entry.get()),
            "output_sigma_factor": 0.1,
            "resize": True,
            "max_patch_size": int(self.patch_entry.get()),
            "split_coeff": True,
            "wrap_kernel": False,
            "desc_pca": 256,
            "desc_npca": 256
        }

        # If params are provided, update the default_params
        if params:
            default_params.update(params)

        # Adjust bbox based on parameters such as scaling
        scale = int(self.scale_entry.get())  #scale is provided through a GUI element
        bbox = (
            int(bbox[0] + (1 - scale) * bbox[2] / 2),  # Center the scaling on the bbox
            int(bbox[1] + (1 - scale) * bbox[3] / 2),
            int(bbox[2] * scale),
            int(bbox[3] * scale)
        )

        # Initialize the KCF tracker
        self.tracker = cv2.legacy.TrackerKCF_create()

        # Assuming a hypothetical method to set parameters (not available in the current OpenCV API)
        # This part is pseudo-code and will not work with standard OpenCV installations
        if hasattr(self.tracker, 'setParams'):
            self.tracker.setParams(default_params)

        self.tracker.init(frame, tuple(map(int, bbox)))
        self.initial_w, self.initial_h = bbox[2], bbox[3]
```

```python
    def track_object(self, frame, bbox, user_params=None):
        """Track object using KCF Tracker with optional user parameters."""
        if bbox:
            if self.tracker is None:
                self.initialize_tracker(frame, bbox, user_params)

            # Update the tracker and get the new bounding box
            success, bbox = self.tracker.update(frame)
            if success:
                x1, y1, w, h = map(int, bbox)
                w, h = self.initial_w, self.initial_h  # Maintain initial dimensions if required
                x2, y2 = x1 + w, y1 + h

                # Calculate and display the center of the bounding box
                center_x = (x1 + x2) // 2
                center_y = (y1 + y2) // 2
                self.center_listbox.insert(tk.END, f"(center_x = {center_x}, center_y = {center_y})")

                return x1, y1, x2, y2
        return None
```

The KCF (Kernelized Correlation Filters) tracker is a sophisticated tracking system designed to maintain the position and size of an object within a video frame over time. This system is particularly well-suited for applications requiring real-time processing, such as surveillance, robotics, and human-computer interaction. The KCF tracker operates by correlating the object's appearance with a filter applied across consecutive video frames, which allows it to efficiently predict the object's new location with a high degree of accuracy.

In the implementation, the initialize_tracker function sets up the KCF tracker using OpenCV's TrackerKCF_create() method. It takes a video frame and a bounding box as input, along with optional user-defined parameters that allow customization of the tracking process. These parameters can adjust aspects such as detection threshold, the influence of the HOG features, and kernel properties, which are essential for tuning the tracker's response to the specific characteristics of the object and the environment.

The function begins by establishing a set of default parameters for the tracker. These include settings for the detection threshold, lambda, sigma, and interpolation factor, among others. These parameters are intended to optimize the tracker's performance by fine-tuning how it processes the object's appearance and motion characteristics. Users have the flexibility to override these defaults by providing their parameters, allowing for dynamic adaptation to different tracking scenarios.

To accommodate different scales of the object being tracked, the function modifies the bounding box based on a scale factor obtained from a GUI entry. This adjustment ensures that the tracker can focus on the most relevant part of the frame, improving both speed and accuracy. Once the bounding box is adjusted, the tracker is initialized with the frame and the modified bounding box.

If initialization succeeds, the function stores the dimensions of the bounding box, which are used later to maintain consistency in the object's apparent size throughout the tracking process. This step is crucial for applications where the object's size provides important context for its interpretation, such as in traffic monitoring systems where the size of a vehicle can indicate its type and speed.

The track_object function is responsible for updating the tracker with each new frame of the video. If the tracker has not been initialized previously, it calls initialize_tracker to set it up. The function then proceeds to update the tracker's position based on the new video frame. Success in this update means the tracker has found the object's new position, and it recalculates the bounding box to reflect this new location.

Upon successful tracking, the function calculates the center of the bounding box, which can be useful for applications needing to know the object's central position, such as in automated targeting systems or for aligning graphics in augmented reality applications.

This center point is also displayed in a list box within the GUI, providing a simple visual feedback mechanism for the user.

This tracking process is repeated for each frame in the video, allowing for continuous monitoring of the object. If at any point the tracking fails (for instance, if the object moves out of frame or becomes occluded), the function can return an indication of this failure, which could then be handled by additional logic to pause tracking, alert the user, or attempt to reacquire the object.

The combination of user-defined parameters and the ability to adapt the scale and position of the bounding box makes this implementation of the KCF tracker highly versatile. It can be adapted for use in diverse environments and applications, providing a robust solution for real-time object tracking.

In conclusion, the KCF tracker in this setup exemplifies a powerful tool in computer vision, integrated within a user-friendly application. By leveraging advanced image processing techniques and providing interfaces for customization and control, it opens up numerous possibilities for automation and interactive technology applications. This integration of sophisticated tracking algorithms with practical, adjustable parameters and real-time feedback exemplifies modern approaches to computer vision challenges.

RUNNING PROGRAM

Run program and choose certain frame by pushing Next Frame button. Then, draw a bounding box rectangle on certain object in the frame and push Next Frame button.

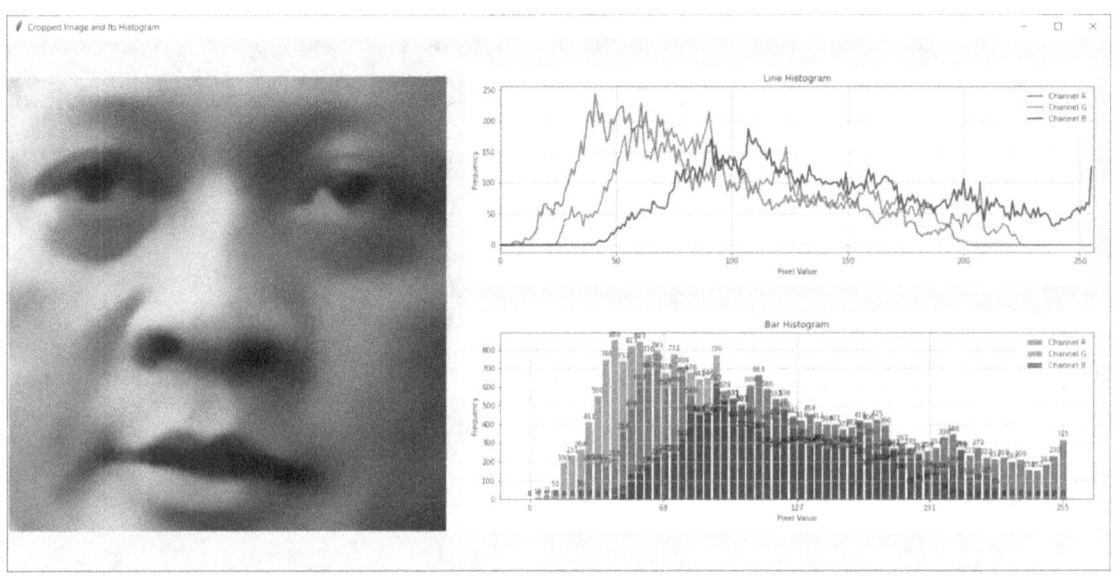

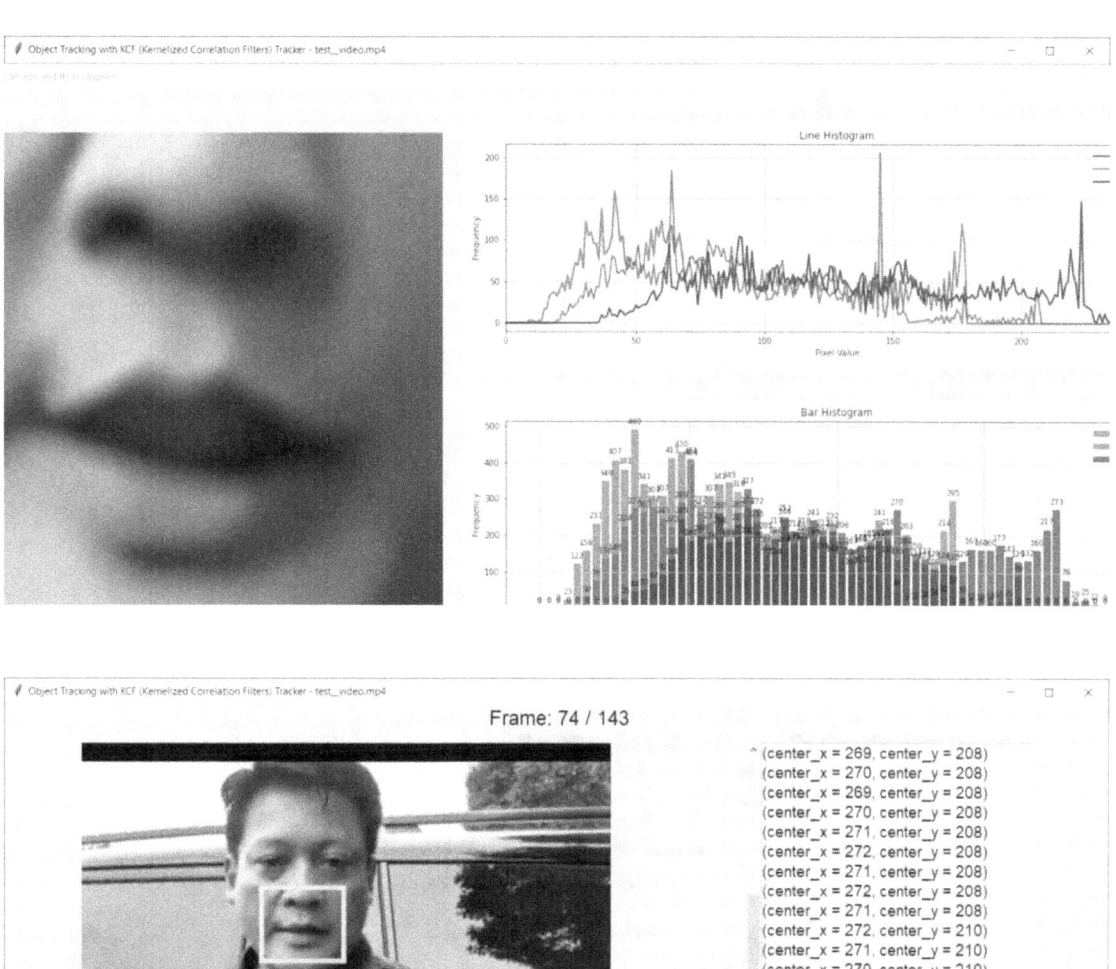

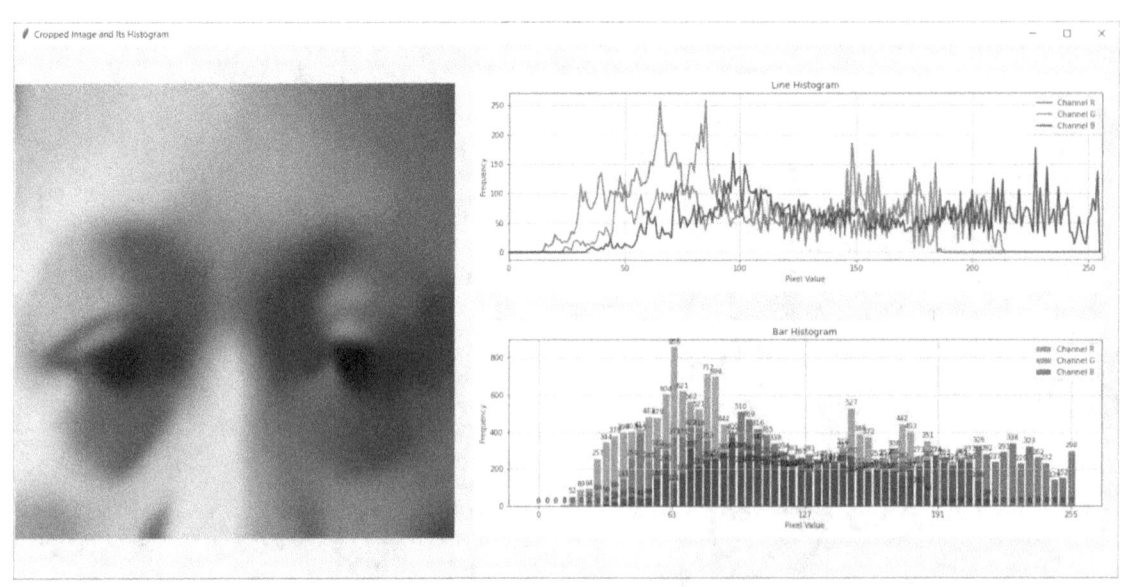

OBJECT TRACKING WITH CSRT (CHANNEL AND SPATIAL RELIABILITY TRACKER)

DESCRIPTION

The CSRT (Channel and Spatial Reliability Tracker) project utilizes a high-performance tracking algorithm that emphasizes accuracy in tracking objects across video frames. Implemented in Python using OpenCV within a Tkinter graphical user interface, this application serves as a robust tool for various tracking tasks where precision and reliability are paramount, such as in surveillance or autonomous vehicle navigation.

The application's user interface is built using Tkinter, offering functionalities like video playback, frame navigation, and interactive controls to manage tracking parameters. The GUI consists of a main window that houses video playback and control panels, providing an intuitive interface for users to interact with the tracker. Users can load videos, control playback, manually adjust the tracking bounding box, and modify tracker settings in real time.

One of the core features of this project is the CSRT tracker's initialization and configuration. The tracker is tailored through a series of parameters that adapt its behavior to different scenarios, ensuring versatility and adaptability. Parameters such as padding, multi-channel scaling, and filter size can be adjusted, allowing the tracker to be fine-tuned for specific tracking challenges.

The initialization of the CSRT tracker involves setting up a bounding box around the object of interest in the first frame, either manually or through automated methods. The tracker uses this initial position to start the tracking process, employing complex algorithms that utilize both channel reliability and spatial information to predict the object's location in subsequent frames.

During tracking, the application updates the position of the bounding box in each frame based on the movements of the tracked object. This is displayed in real-time on the video playback interface, where users can visually monitor the tracker's performance. The tracker's ability to adapt to changes in object appearance, lighting, and occlusions makes it particularly effective in real-world applications.

Besides tracking, the application offers additional functionalities like zoom controls and video frame navigation, which enhance the user's ability to interact with the video and focus on details relevant to the tracking process. These features are particularly useful in scenarios where precise monitoring of object movements is required.

The integration of various image filters and transformations provides users with tools to preprocess video frames within the application. Filters such as Gaussian blur, median filtering, and adaptive thresholding can be applied to frames before tracking, which can help in enhancing the tracker's accuracy and performance in challenging conditions.

For advanced analysis, the application includes functionalities to examine specific details within a tracked frame. This includes generating histograms of color distributions and applying complex image transformations like wavelet transforms, which can be useful for detailed image analysis and feature extraction in academic and research settings.

To assist with debugging and performance optimization, the application provides a comprehensive logging and error-handling framework that captures and displays critical information about the tracker's operation. This can include data on tracking errors, parameter adjustments, and system statuses, which are invaluable for refining the tracker's settings and improving its robustness.

Overall, the CSRT Tracker application exemplifies a sophisticated integration of image processing algorithms and user interface design, delivering a powerful tool for video analysis and object tracking. It showcases the potential of combining advanced computer vision techniques with user-friendly software design to create applications that are both powerful and accessible to a wide range of users.

TRACKING OBJECT

```python
def initialize_tracker(self, frame, bbox, params=None):
    """Initialize the CSRT tracker with possible user-defined parameters."""

    # Read scale factor from a GUI entry; ensure it is a float
    scale = float(self.scale_entry.get())

    # Adjust bbox based on the scaling parameter
    bbox = (
        int(bbox[0] + (1 - scale) * bbox[2] / 2),  # Center the scaling on the bbox
        int(bbox[1] + (1 - scale) * bbox[3] / 2),
        int(bbox[2] * scale),
```

```python
            int(bbox[3] * scale)
        )

        # Initialize the CSRT tracker
        self.tracker = cv2.legacy.TrackerCSRT_create()

        # Initialize the tracker with the frame and adjusted bbox
        success = self.tracker.init(frame, tuple(map(int, bbox)))
        if not success:
            print("Tracker initialization failed.")
            return False

        self.initial_w, self.initial_h = bbox[2], bbox[3]
        return True

    def track_object(self, frame, bbox, user_params=None):
        """Track object using CSRT Tracker with optional user parameters."""
        if not self.tracker:
            if not self.initialize_tracker(frame, bbox, user_params):
                return None

        # Update the tracker and get the new bounding box
        success, bbox = self.tracker.update(frame)
        if success:
            x1, y1, w, h = map(int, bbox)
            x2, y2 = x1 + w, y1 + h

            # Calculate and display the center of the bounding box
            center_x = (x1 + x2) // 2
            center_y = (y1 + y2) // 2
            if hasattr(self, 'center_listbox'):
                self.center_listbox.insert(tk.END, f"(center_x = {center_x}, center_y = {center_y})")

            return (x1, y1, x2, y2)
        return None
```

The CSRT (Consensus-based Sequential Tracking and Detection) Tracker is designed for high accuracy video tracking which makes it ideal for applications where precise tracking of objects through complex sequences is required, such as in sports analytics or for tracking vehicles in traffic scenes. This tracker is part of an application implemented using Python with OpenCV, integrated into a user-friendly graphical interface using Tkinter.

The interface allows users to interact directly with the video, initializing tracking, adjusting parameters, and scrutinizing tracking results frame by frame.

Initialization of the CSRT tracker within the application involves setting up the tracking parameters which can be user-defined or set to defaults. The key part of the setup is the definition of the bounding box that identifies the target object's initial position. Users can input the scale factor directly in the graphical user interface, which adjusts the size of the bounding box to ensure that the tracker focuses on an area that is large enough to include the entire object but not so large that it includes excessive background information which might confuse the tracker.

The actual initialization call creates an instance of the CSRT tracker with the specified bounding box and parameters. The process involves preprocessing the selected region of the initial frame using techniques such as histogram equalization to improve the robustness of the tracker against changes in lighting and appearance. If the initialization fails, the application notifies the user, allowing for adjustments or reselection of the tracking area.

During the tracking phase, the CSRT tracker employs a sophisticated algorithm that evaluates multiple hypotheses of the object's potential location in subsequent frames, based on the spatial reliability which assesses the quality of the tracker's response. It uses channel reliability to dynamically adjust the weights of different channels of the histogram-based model, enhancing its adaptability to appearance changes due to occlusion, camera motion, or object deformation.

Each time a new frame is processed, the tracker updates the position of the bounding box. This is displayed in real time on the application's interface, providing immediate visual feedback to the user. The center of the bounding box is calculated and displayed, which is particularly useful for applications requiring data on the trajectory or motion patterns of the tracked object.

In scenarios where the tracker loses the object, such as when it moves out of frame or is completely occluded, the tracker's performance can degrade, and tracking may fail. This state is also handled within the system by allowing users to reinitialize the tracking with a new bounding box, thus providing robustness in long-duration tracking scenarios.

Beyond tracking, the application offers tools for detailed analysis, such as zoom features and frame-by-frame navigation. These features are crucial for detailed post-processing analysis, allowing users to study specific segments of video footage for behaviors or events that are not easily observable in real-time playback.

The interface includes functionalities to apply various image filters and transformations which can preprocess the frames fed into the tracker. This preprocessing can enhance tracking accuracy under difficult visual conditions like low light or high noise environments. Options include filters such as Gaussian blur and adaptive thresholding, as well as more complex transformations like wavelet transforms.

For a more technical insight into the tracking process, the application provides histogram displays of the color distributions within the tracked region. This feature helps in understanding how the tracker perceives the object and its background, which can be essential for tuning the tracker settings for specific environments or types of objects.

Overall, the CSRT Tracker application encapsulates a complex computer vision functionality within a user-friendly interface that caters to both novice users and professionals. It demonstrates the practical application of advanced object tracking technologies, bridging the gap between high-level research and real-world application needs.

RUNNING PROGRAM

Run program and choose certain frame by pushing Next Frame button. Then, draw a bounding box rectangle on certain object in the frame and push Next Frame button.

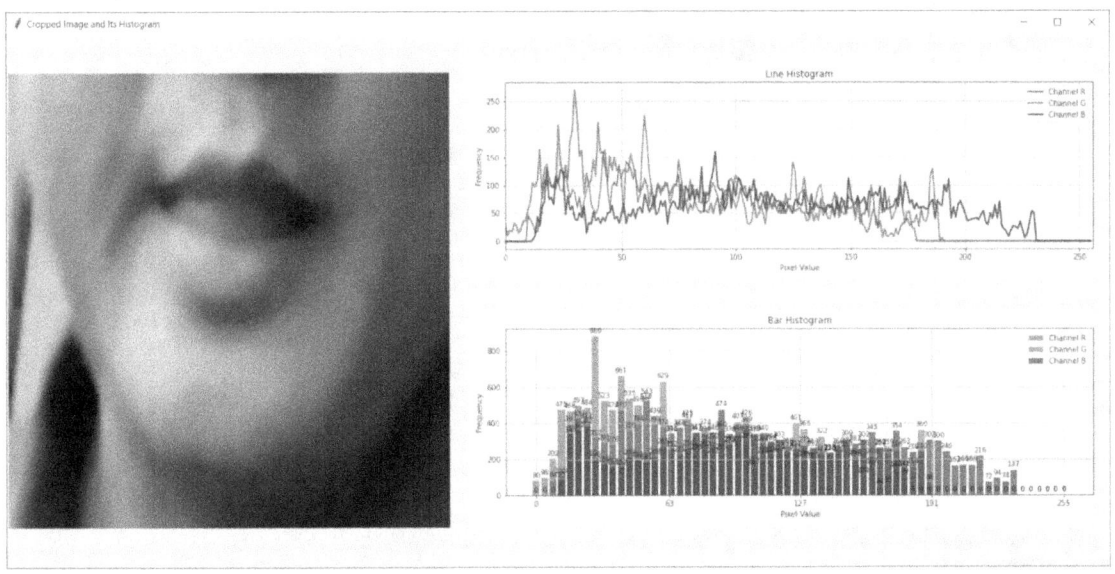

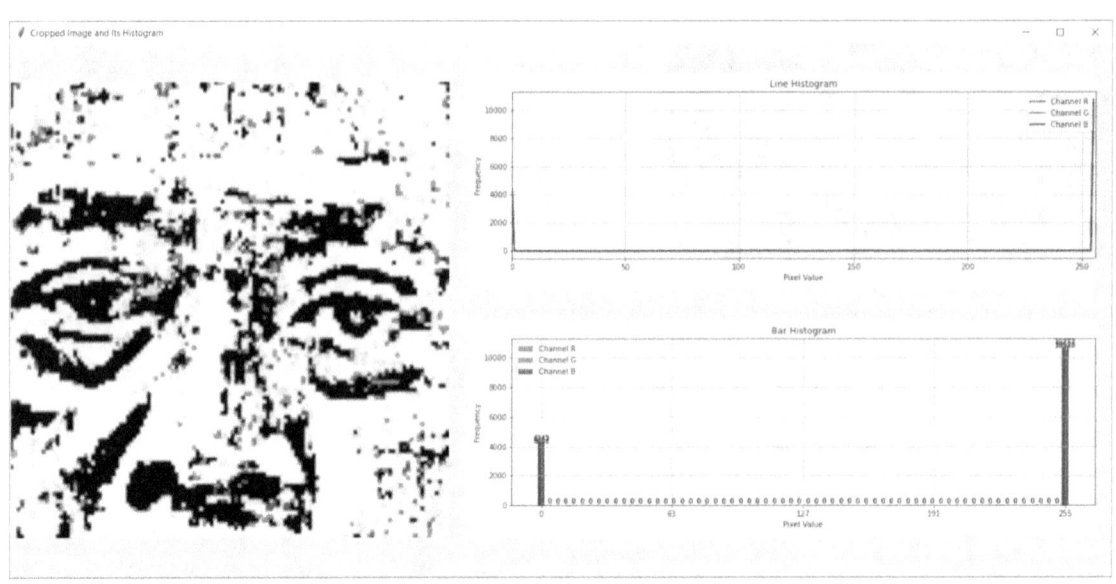

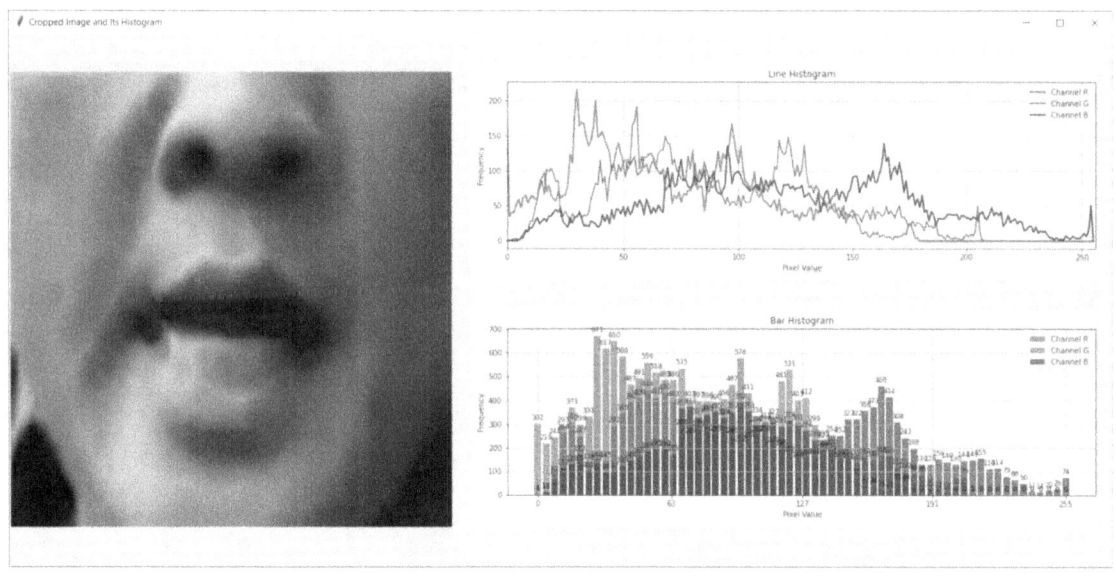

SOURCE CODE

```python
#csrt_tracker.py
import tkinter as tk
from tkinter import ttk
from tkinter import filedialog
from PIL import Image, ImageTk
import imageio
import cv2
import numpy as np
import matplotlib.pyplot as plt
import pywt

class CSRTTracker:
    def __init__(self, master):
        self.master = master
        self.master.title("Object Tracking with CSRT (Channel and Spatial Reliability Tracker)")
        self.file_name = ""
        self.set_window_title()  # Set window title initially

        self.frame_number_label = tk.Label(master, text="Frame: 0")
        self.frame_number_label.pack()
```

```python
        self.video = None
        self.video_path = None
        self.paused = False
        self.zoom_scale = tk.IntVar(value=1)
        self.frame_index = 0
        self.bbox = None
        self.bbox2 = None
        self.tracking_started = False  # Initialize tracking_started to False
        self.prev_frame_gray = None
        self.tracker = None
        self.initial_w = None
        self.initial_h = None
        self.bbox_rect = None  # Initialize bbox_rect attribute to None
        self.frame_processing = False  # Initialize frame_processing attribute to False

        # Available filters
        self.filters = ["None", "Gaussian", "Mean", "Median", "Bilateral Filtering",
                        "Non-local Means Denoising", "Anisotropic Diffusion",
                        "Total Variation Denoising", "Wiener Filter",
                        "Adaptive Thresholding", "Haar Wavelet Transform",
                        "Daubechies Wavelet Transform"]

        self.create_widgets()

    def create_widgets(self):
        # Panel for video display
        video_panel = tk.Frame(self.master)
        video_panel.pack(padx=10, pady=10)

        # Canvas to display the original video
        canvas_width = 800
        canvas_height = 500
        self.canvas = tk.Canvas(video_panel, width=canvas_width, height=canvas_height)
        self.canvas.pack(side="left", fill="both", expand=True)
        self.canvas.bind("<MouseWheel>", self.on_mousewheel)
        self.canvas.bind("<ButtonPress-1>", self.on_press)
        self.canvas.bind("<B1-Motion>", self.on_drag)
        self.canvas.bind("<ButtonRelease-1>", self.on_release)  # Bind ButtonRelease event

        # List box to display center coordinates
        self.center_listbox = tk.Listbox(video_panel, width=30, height=20, font=("Helvetica", 14))
        self.center_listbox.pack(side="right", fill="y")
        # Scrollbar for the listbox
```

```python
        scrollbar = tk.Scrollbar(video_panel, orient="vertical")
        scrollbar.pack(side="left", fill="y")
        scrollbar.config(command=self.center_listbox.yview)

        # Attach scrollbar to listbox
        self.center_listbox.config(yscrollcommand=scrollbar.set)

        # Panel for control buttons
        control_panel = tk.Frame(self.master)
        control_panel.pack(padx=10, pady=(0, 10), fill="x")

        # Button to open a video file
        self.open_button = tk.Button(control_panel, text="Open Video", command=self.open_video)
        self.open_button.grid(row=0, column=0, padx=10, pady=5)

        # Combobox for selecting zoom scale
        self.zoom_combobox = ttk.Combobox(control_panel, textvariable=self.zoom_scale, values=list(range(1, 11)))
        self.zoom_combobox.grid(row=0, column=1, padx=10, pady=5)
        self.zoom_combobox.bind("<<ComboboxSelected>>", self.update_zoom)

        # Button to play/pause the video
        self.play_button = tk.Button(control_panel, text="Play/Pause", command=self.toggle_play_pause)
        self.play_button.grid(row=0, column=2, padx=10, pady=5)

        # Button to stop the video
        self.stop_button = tk.Button(control_panel, text="Stop", command=self.stop_video)
        self.stop_button.grid(row=0, column=3, padx=10, pady=5)

        # Button to navigate to the previous frame
        self.prev_frame_button = tk.Button(control_panel, text="Previous Frame", command=self.prev_frame)
        self.prev_frame_button.grid(row=0, column=4, padx=10, pady=5)

        # Button to navigate to the next frame
        self.next_frame_button = tk.Button(control_panel, text="Next Frame", command=self.next_frame)
        self.next_frame_button.grid(row=0, column=5, padx=10, pady=5)

        # Button to clear the listbox
        self.clear_button = tk.Button(control_panel, text="Clear Listbox", command=self.clear_listbox)
        self.clear_button.grid(row=0, column=6, padx=10, pady=5)

        # Label and entry for specifying scale
```

```python
        self.scale_label = tk.Label(control_panel, text="Scale:")
        self.scale_label.grid(row=0, column=7, padx=10, pady=5, sticky="e")
        self.scale_default = tk.StringVar(value="1")
        self.scale_entry = ttk.Entry(control_panel, textvariable=self.scale_default)
        self.scale_entry.grid(row=0, column=8, padx=10, pady=5, sticky="w")
        self.scale_entry.bind("<Return>", lambda event: self.toggle_play_pause())

        # Combobox for selecting filters
        self.filter_combobox = ttk.Combobox(control_panel, values=self.filters)
        self.filter_combobox.grid(row=0, column=9, padx=10, pady=5)
        self.filter_combobox.current(0)  # Set default value

    def open_video(self):
        self.video_path = filedialog.askopenfilename(filetypes=[("Video files", "*.mp4;*.avi;*.mkv;*.wmv")])
        if self.video_path:
            self.video = imageio.get_reader(self.video_path)
            self.file_name = self.video_path.split('/')[-1]
            self.set_window_title()
            self.play_video()

    def play_video(self):
        if self.video:
            self.paused = False
            self.tracking_started = True
            self.show_frame()

    def stop_video(self):
        self.paused = True
        self.frame_index = 0
        self.bbox = None
        self.tracker = None  # Reset tracker
        self.initial_w = None  # Reset width
        self.initial_h = None  # Reset height
        self.show_frame()

    def toggle_play_pause(self):
        self.paused = not self.paused
        if not self.paused:
            if self.bbox is not None:
                self.tracking_started = True
            self.play_video()

    def update_zoom(self, event=None):
        self.show_frame()

    def initialize_tracker(self, frame, bbox, params=None):
        """Initialize the CSRT tracker with possible user-defined parameters."""
```

```python
        # Read scale factor from a GUI entry; ensure it is a float
        scale = float(self.scale_entry.get())

        # Adjust bbox based on the scaling parameter
        bbox = (
            int(bbox[0] + (1 - scale) * bbox[2] / 2),  # Center the scaling on the bbox
            int(bbox[1] + (1 - scale) * bbox[3] / 2),
            int(bbox[2] * scale),
            int(bbox[3] * scale)
        )

        # Initialize the CSRT tracker
        self.tracker = cv2.legacy.TrackerCSRT_create()

        # Initialize the tracker with the frame and adjusted bbox
        success = self.tracker.init(frame, tuple(map(int, bbox)))
        if not success:
            print("Tracker initialization failed.")
            return False

        self.initial_w, self.initial_h = bbox[2], bbox[3]
        return True

    def track_object(self, frame, bbox, user_params=None):
        """Track object using CSRT Tracker with optional user parameters."""
        if not self.tracker:
            if not self.initialize_tracker(frame, bbox, user_params):
                return None

        # Update the tracker and get the new bounding box
        success, bbox = self.tracker.update(frame)
        if success:
            x1, y1, w, h = map(int, bbox)
            x2, y2 = x1 + w, y1 + h

            # Calculate and display the center of the bounding box
            center_x = (x1 + x2) // 2
            center_y = (y1 + y2) // 2
            if hasattr(self, 'center_listbox'):
                self.center_listbox.insert(tk.END, f"(center_x = {center_x}, center_y = {center_y})")

            return (x1, y1, x2, y2)
        return None

    def update_bbox_rectangle(self, bbox):
```

```python
        if bbox is not None:
            x1, y1, x2, y2 = map(int, bbox)
            if self.bbox_rect is not None:
                self.canvas.coords(self.bbox_rect, x1, y1, x2, y2)
                self.canvas.tag_raise(self.bbox_rect)  # Raise the bounding box to the front
            else:
                self.bbox_rect = self.canvas.create_rectangle(x1, y1, x2, y2, outline='#fc3d3d', width=8, tags="bbox")

    def show_frame(self):
        if self.video:
            if not self.paused:
                if 0 <= self.frame_index < len(self.video):
                    if not self.frame_processing:  # Check if the frame is already being processed
                        try:
                            self.frame_processing = True  # Set frame_processing flag to True to indicate frame processing

                            frame = self.video.get_data(self.frame_index)
                            frame = cv2.cvtColor(frame, cv2.COLOR_RGB2BGR)

                            if self.bbox is not None:
                                if not self.tracking_started:
                                    self.tracking_started = True

                                self.bbox = self.track_object(frame, self.bbox)
                                if self.bbox:
                                    frame = cv2.cvtColor(frame, cv2.COLOR_BGR2RGB)
                                    frame = Image.fromarray(frame)
                                    frame = frame.resize((frame.width * self.zoom_scale.get(), frame.height * self.zoom_scale.get()))
                                    photo = ImageTk.PhotoImage(frame)
                                    self.photo = photo
                                    self.canvas.delete("video")
                                    self.canvas.create_image(0, 0, anchor="nw", image=photo, tags="video")

                                    self.update_bbox_rectangle(self.bbox)

                            else:
                                frame = cv2.cvtColor(frame, cv2.COLOR_BGR2RGB)
                                frame = Image.fromarray(frame)
                                frame = frame.resize((frame.width * self.zoom_scale.get(), frame.height * self.zoom_scale.get()))
                                photo = ImageTk.PhotoImage(frame)
                                self.photo = photo
                                self.canvas.delete("video")
```

```python
                        self.canvas.create_image(0, 0, anchor="nw", 
image=photo, tags="video")

                        self.frame_number_label.config(text=f"Frame: 
{self.frame_index} / {self.video.count_frames()}", font=("Helvetica", 18))

                        self.frame_index += 1

                except Exception as e:
                    print("Error: ", e)
                finally:
                    self.frame_processing = False  # Reset frame_processing 
flag to False after processing the frame

    def on_mousewheel(self, event):
        direction = event.delta // 120
        current_value = int(self.zoom_scale.get())
        if direction == 1 and current_value < 10:
            current_value += 1
        elif direction == -1 and current_value > 1:
            current_value -= 1
        self.zoom_scale.set(current_value)
        self.update_zoom()

    def on_press(self, event):
        self.tracker = None
        self.start_x = self.canvas.canvasx(event.x)
        self.start_y = self.canvas.canvasy(event.y)
        # Clear the previous bounding box if it exists
        if self.bbox_rect:
            self.canvas.delete(self.bbox_rect)
            self.bbox_rect = None
        self.bbox = None
        self.bbox2 = None

    def on_drag(self, event):
        # Update the endpoint of the rectangle as the mouse moves
        cur_x = self.canvas.canvasx(event.x)
        cur_y = self.canvas.canvasy(event.y)

        # Define the coordinates correctly ensuring x1 < x2 and y1 < y2
        x1, y1 = min(self.start_x, cur_x), min(self.start_y, cur_y)
        x2, y2 = max(self.start_x, cur_x), max(self.start_y, cur_y)

        # Update dimensions for tracking
        self.initial_w = x2 - x1
        self.initial_h = y2 - y1
        self.bbox = (x1, y1, self.initial_w, self.initial_h)
```

```python
            self.bbox2 = (self.start_x, self.start_y, cur_x, cur_y)

            # Update or create a rectangle on the canvas
            if self.bbox_rect:
                self.canvas.coords(self.bbox_rect, x1, y1, x2, y2)
            else:
                self.bbox_rect = self.canvas.create_rectangle(x1, y1, x2, y2, 
outline="cyan", width=6)     
                
    def prev_frame(self):
        if self.frame_index > 0:
            self.frame_index -= 1
            self.show_frame()

    def next_frame(self):
        if self.video and self.frame_index < len(self.video) - 1:
            self.show_frame()

    def clear_listbox(self):
        self.center_listbox.delete(0, tk.END)
            
    def set_window_title(self):
        if self.file_name:
            self.master.title(f"Object Tracking with CSRT (Channel and Spatial 
Reliability Tracker) - {self.file_name}")
            self.master.title_font = ("Helvetica", 16, "bold")
        else:
            self.master.title("Object Tracking with CSRT (Channel and Spatial 
Reliability Tracker)")
            
    def on_release(self, self, event):
        self.analyze_histogram()  # Call analyze_histogram() method when the mouse 
button is released
        
    def analyze_histogram(self):
        if self.bbox2 is not None and self.video:
            x1, y1, x2, y2 = map(int, self.bbox2)
            if x1 != x2 and y1 != y2:
                try:
                    frame = self.video.get_data(self.frame_index)
                    # Ensure the bounding box is within the frame boundaries
                    h, w, _ = frame.shape
                    x1, x2 = max(0, min(x1, w)), max(0, min(x2, w))
                    y1, y2 = max(0, min(y1, h)), max(0, min(y2, h))
                    
                    # Ensure x1 < x2 and y1 < y2
                    x1, x2 = sorted([x1, x2])
```

```python
                    y1, y2 = sorted([y1, y2])

                    cropped_frame = frame[y1:y2, x1:x2]
                    if cropped_frame.size > 0:
                        cropped_frame = cv2.cvtColor(cropped_frame, cv2.COLOR_BGR2RGB)

                        # Get selected filter from combobox
                        selected_filter = self.filter_combobox.get()
                        # Apply selected filter
                        filtered_frame = self.apply_filter(selected_filter, cropped_frame)

                        self.create_popup_window(filtered_frame)
                        self.display_cropped_image(filtered_frame)
                        self.display_histograms(filtered_frame)
                    else:
                        print("Cropped frame is empty.")
                except Exception as e:
                    print("Failed to process frame:", e)
            else:
                print("Bounding box dimensions are zero or negative.")

    def create_popup_window(self, cropped_frame):
        self.popup_window = tk.Toplevel(self.master)
        self.popup_window.title("Cropped Image and Its Histogram")
        self.popup_window.geometry("1500x700")


    def display_cropped_image(self, cropped_frame):
        cropped_frame_frame = tk.Frame(self.popup_window)
        cropped_frame_frame.pack(side="left")

        cropped_frame_rgb = cv2.cvtColor(cropped_frame, cv2.COLOR_BGR2RGB)
        cropped_img = Image.fromarray(cropped_frame_rgb)
        cropped_img = cropped_img.resize((600, 600))

        cropped_photo = ImageTk.PhotoImage(cropped_img)
        cropped_canvas = tk.Canvas(cropped_frame_frame, width=600, height=600)
        cropped_canvas.pack(side="left", anchor="nw")
        cropped_canvas.create_image(0, 0, anchor="nw", image=cropped_photo)
        cropped_canvas.image = cropped_photo

    def display_histograms(self, cropped_frame):
        histograms_frame = tk.Frame(self.popup_window)
        histograms_frame.pack(side="right", padx=20)
```

```python
        self.display_line_histogram(cropped_frame, histograms_frame)
        self.display_bar_histogram(cropped_frame, histograms_frame)

    def display_line_histogram(self, cropped_frame, histograms_frame):
        line_histogram_frame = tk.Frame(histograms_frame)
        line_histogram_frame.pack(side="top", pady=10)

        plt.figure(figsize=(12, 4))
        color = ('r', 'g', 'b')
        for i, col in enumerate(color):
            histr = cv2.calcHist([cropped_frame], [i], None, [256], [0, 256])
            plt.plot(histr, color=col, label=f'Channel {col.upper()}', linewidth=2)
            plt.xlim([0, 256])
        plt.title('Line Histogram')
        plt.xlabel('Pixel Value')
        plt.ylabel('Frequency')
        plt.tight_layout()
        plt.grid(True)
        plt.legend()

        line_histogram_img = self.plot_to_image(plt)
        self.display_histogram_image(line_histogram_frame, line_histogram_img)

    def display_bar_histogram(self, cropped_frame, histograms_frame):
        bar_histogram_frame = tk.Frame(histograms_frame)
        bar_histogram_frame.pack(side="bottom", pady=10)

        plt.figure(figsize=(12, 4))
        color = ('r', 'g', 'b')
        for i, col in enumerate(color):
            hist_range = (0, 256)
            hist_counts, _ = np.histogram(cropped_frame[:, :, i], bins=64, range=hist_range)
            plt.bar(np.arange(64), hist_counts, color=col, alpha=0.7, label=f'Channel {col.upper()}')
            for index, value in enumerate(hist_counts):
                plt.text(index, value + 10, str(int(value)), ha='center', va='bottom', fontsize=9)

        plt.title('Bar Histogram')
        plt.xlabel('Pixel Value')
        plt.ylabel('Frequency')
        plt.xticks(np.linspace(0, 63, num=5), np.linspace(0, 255, num=5, dtype=int))
        # Adjust x-axis ticks
        plt.tight_layout()
        plt.grid(True)
        plt.legend()
```

```python
        bar_histogram_img = self.plot_to_image(plt)
        self.display_histogram_image(bar_histogram_frame, bar_histogram_img)

    def display_histogram_image(self, parent_frame, img):
        histogram_photo = ImageTk.PhotoImage(image=img)
        histogram_canvas = tk.Canvas(parent_frame, width=900, height=300)
        histogram_canvas.pack(side="bottom", anchor="se")
        histogram_canvas.create_image(0, 0, anchor="nw", image=histogram_photo)
        histogram_canvas.image = histogram_photo

    def plot_histogram_bar_to_image(self, image):
        # Calculate histogram for each channel
        histograms = []
        for i in range(3):
            hist_range = (0, 256)
            hist_counts, _ = np.histogram(image[:, :, i], bins=64, range=hist_range)  # Adjust bins to 64
            histograms.append(hist_counts)

        # Extracting only 64 bins from the histogram
        num_bins = 64  # Adjusted to 64 bins

        # Generating colors for each channel
        colors = ['red', 'green', 'blue']

        plt.figure()
        for i, histogram in enumerate(histograms):
            # Normalize the histogram counts for better visualization
            hist_counts = histogram / np.sum(histogram)
            # Setting the color for each channel
            plt.bar(np.arange(num_bins), hist_counts[:num_bins], color=colors[i], alpha=0.7, label=f'Channel {["Red", "Green", "Blue"][i]}')

        plt.xlabel('Pixel Value')
        plt.ylabel('Normalized Frequency')
        plt.title('RGB Channel Histograms')
        plt.grid(True)
        plt.tight_layout()
        plt.legend()

        # Convert the histogram bar graph to an image
        histogram_bar_img = self.plot_to_image(plt)
        histogram_bar_photo = ImageTk.PhotoImage(image=histogram_bar_img)

        return histogram_bar_photo

    def plot_to_image(self, plt):
        plt.savefig('temp_plot.png')
```

```python
        img = Image.open('temp_plot.png')
        return img

    def apply_filter(self, filter_name, frame):
        if filter_name == "None":
            return frame
        elif filter_name == "Gaussian":
            return cv2.GaussianBlur(frame, (5, 5), 0)
        elif filter_name == "Mean":
            return cv2.blur(frame, (5, 5))
        elif filter_name == "Median":
            return cv2.medianBlur(frame, 5)
        elif filter_name == "Bilateral Filtering":
            return cv2.bilateralFilter(frame, 9, 75, 75)
        elif filter_name == "Non-local Means Denoising":
            return cv2.fastNlMeansDenoisingColored(frame, None, 10, 10, 7, 21)
        elif filter_name == "Anisotropic Diffusion":
            return self.anisotropic_diffusion(frame)
        elif filter_name == "Total Variation Denoising":
            return self.total_variation_denoising(frame)
        elif filter_name == "Wiener Filter":
            return self.wiener_filter(frame)
        elif filter_name == "Adaptive Thresholding":
            return self.adaptive_threshold_each_channel(frame)
        elif filter_name == "Haar Wavelet Transform":
            return self.haar_wavelet_transform(frame)
        elif filter_name == "Daubechies Wavelet Transform":
            return self.daubechies_wavelet_transform(frame)
        else:
            return frame  # Default: return original frame if filter not found

    def wiener_filter(self, frame, kernel_size=(5, 5), noise_var=0.01):
        # Check if frame is None
        if frame is None:
            print("Error: Input frame is None.")
            return None

        # Check if frame is a valid numpy array
        if not isinstance(frame, np.ndarray):
            print("Error: Input frame is not a numpy array.")
            return None

        # Check if frame is an empty array
        if frame.size == 0:
            print("Error: Input frame is empty.")
            return None

        # Check if frame is in BGR color space
```

```python
        if frame.shape[-1] != 3:
            print("Error: Input frame is not in BGR color space.")
            return None

        # Apply Wiener filter
        filtered_frame = cv2.medianBlur(frame, kernel_size[0])  # Use kernel_size[0] as the kernel size
        filtered_frame = cv2.fastNlMeansDenoising(filtered_frame, h=noise_var)
        return filtered_frame

    def adaptive_threshold_each_channel(self, frame):
        # Split the frame into individual channels
        b, g, r = cv2.split(frame)

        # Apply adaptive thresholding to each channel separately
        b_thresh = cv2.adaptiveThreshold(b, 255, cv2.ADAPTIVE_THRESH_GAUSSIAN_C, cv2.THRESH_BINARY, 11, 2)
        g_thresh = cv2.adaptiveThreshold(g, 255, cv2.ADAPTIVE_THRESH_GAUSSIAN_C, cv2.THRESH_BINARY, 11, 2)
        r_thresh = cv2.adaptiveThreshold(r, 255, cv2.ADAPTIVE_THRESH_GAUSSIAN_C, cv2.THRESH_BINARY, 11, 2)

        # Merge the thresholded channels back together
        return cv2.merge([b_thresh, g_thresh, r_thresh])

    def haar_wavelet_transform(self, frame):
        # Split the frame into its individual color channels
        b, g, r = cv2.split(frame)

        # Perform the wavelet transform on each channel separately
        b_coeffs = pywt.dwt2(b, 'haar')
        g_coeffs = pywt.dwt2(g, 'haar')
        r_coeffs = pywt.dwt2(r, 'haar')

        # Reconstruct the channels from the coefficients
        b_reconstructed = pywt.idwt2(b_coeffs, 'haar')
        g_reconstructed = pywt.idwt2(g_coeffs, 'haar')
        r_reconstructed = pywt.idwt2(r_coeffs, 'haar')

        # Clip the values to ensure they are within the valid range
        b_reconstructed = np.clip(b_reconstructed, 0, 255).astype(np.uint8)
        g_reconstructed = np.clip(g_reconstructed, 0, 255).astype(np.uint8)
        r_reconstructed = np.clip(r_reconstructed, 0, 255).astype(np.uint8)

        # Merge the channels back together
        return cv2.merge([b_reconstructed, g_reconstructed, r_reconstructed])

    def daubechies_wavelet_transform(self, frame):
```

```python
        # Split the frame into its individual color channels
        b, g, r = cv2.split(frame)

        # Choose the wavelet function (Daubechies 5)
        wavelet = 'db5'

        # Perform the wavelet transform on each channel separately
        b_coeffs = pywt.dwt2(b, wavelet)
        g_coeffs = pywt.dwt2(g, wavelet)
        r_coeffs = pywt.dwt2(r, wavelet)

        # Reconstruct the channels from the coefficients
        b_reconstructed = pywt.idwt2(b_coeffs, wavelet)
        g_reconstructed = pywt.idwt2(g_coeffs, wavelet)
        r_reconstructed = pywt.idwt2(r_coeffs, wavelet)

        # Clip the values to ensure they are within the valid range
        b_reconstructed = np.clip(b_reconstructed, 0, 255).astype(np.uint8)
        g_reconstructed = np.clip(g_reconstructed, 0, 255).astype(np.uint8)
        r_reconstructed = np.clip(r_reconstructed, 0, 255).astype(np.uint8)

        # Merge the channels back together
        return cv2.merge([b_reconstructed, g_reconstructed, r_reconstructed])

    def anisotropic_diffusion(self, img):
        return cv2.fastNlMeansDenoisingColored(img, None, 10, 10, 7, 21)

    def apply_total_variation_denoising_channel(self, channel, weight, iterations):
        # Initialize the result with the original channel
        result = channel.copy().astype(np.float64)  # Convert to float64

        # Perform total variation denoising
        for _ in range(iterations):
            # Compute the gradient of the channel
            dx = cv2.Sobel(result, cv2.CV_64F, 1, 0, ksize=3)
            dy = cv2.Sobel(result, cv2.CV_64F, 0, 1, ksize=3)

            # Update the channel using the gradient and the weight
            result -= weight * np.sqrt(dx**2 + dy**2)

        # Clip the values to ensure they are within the valid range
        result = np.clip(result, 0, 255).astype(np.uint8)

        return result

    def total_variation_denoising(self, img, weight=0.01, iterations=20):
        # Split the image into its individual color channels
        b, g, r = cv2.split(img)
```

```
        # Apply total variation denoising to each channel separately
        b_denoised = self.apply_total_variation_denoising_channel(b, weight, iterations)
        g_denoised = self.apply_total_variation_denoising_channel(g, weight, iterations)
        r_denoised = self.apply_total_variation_denoising_channel(r, weight, iterations)

        # Merge the denoised channels back together
        return cv2.merge([b_denoised, g_denoised, r_denoised])

def main():
    root = tk.Tk()
    app = CSRTTracker(root)
    root.mainloop()

if __name__ == "__main__":
    main()
```

Bibliography

Vivian Siahaan and Rismon Hasiholan Sianipar. *TKINTER, DATA SCIENCE, AND MACHINE LEARNING*. North Sumatera: Balige Publishing, 2023.

Vivian Siahaan and Rismon Hasiholan Sianipar. *DATA VISUALIZATION, TIME-SERIES FORECASTING, AND PREDICTION USING MACHINE LEARNING WITH TKINTER*. North Sumatera: Balige Publishing, 2023.

Vivian Siahaan and Rismon Hasiholan Sianipar. *TIME-SERIES WEATHER FORECASTING AND PREDICTION USING MACHINE LEARNING WITH TKINTER*. North Sumatera: Balige Publishing, 2023.

Vivian Siahaan and Rismon Hasiholan Sianipar. DATA VISUALIZATION, TIME-SERIES FORECASTING, AND PREDICTION USING MACHINE LEARNING WITH TKINTER. North Sumatera: Balige Publishing, 2023.

Vivian Siahaan and Rismon Hasiholan Sianipar. START FROM SCRATCH DIGITAL SIGNAL PROCESSING WITH TKINTER. North Sumatera: Balige Publishing, 2023.

Vivian Siahaan and Rismon Hasiholan Sianipar. START FROM SCRATCH DIGITAL IMAGE PROCESSING WITH TKINTER. North Sumatera: Balige Publishing, 2023.

Vivian Siahaan and Rismon Hasiholan Sianipar. START FROM SCRATCH DIGITAL IMAGE PROCESSING WITH TKINTER. North Sumatera: Balige Publishing, 2023.

Vivian Siahaan and Rismon Hasiholan Sianipar. IMAGE DENOISING, EDGE DETECTION, AND SEGMENTATION WITH TKINTER. North Sumatera: Balige Publishing, 2023.

Vivian Siahaan and Rismon Hasiholan Sianipar. DIGITAL VIDEO PROCESSING PROJECTS USING PYTHON AND TKINTER. North Sumatera: Balige Publishing, 2024.

Vivian Siahaan and Rismon Hasiholan Sianipar. FRAME ANALYSIS AND PROCESSING IN DIGITAL VIDEO USING PYTHON AND TKINTER. North Sumatera: Balige Publishing, 2024.

Vivian Siahaan and Rismon Hasiholan Sianipar. MOTION ANALYSIS AND OBJECT TRACKING USING PYTHON AND TKINTER. North Sumatera: Balige Publishing, 2024.

Vivian Siahaan and Rismon Hasiholan Sianipar. FRAME FILTERING AND EDGES-DETECTION USING PYTHON AND TKINTER. North Sumatera: Balige Publishing, 2024.

Vivian Siahaan and Rismon Hasiholan Sianipar. OPTICAL FLOW ANALYSIS AND MOTION ESTIMATION IN DIGITAL VIDEO WITH PYTHON AND TKINTER. North Sumatera: Balige Publishing, 2024.

Vivian Siahaan and Rismon Hasiholan Sianipar. GRADIENT-BASED BLOCK MATCHING MOTION ESTIMATION AND OBJECT TRACKING WITH PYTHON AND TKINTER. North Sumatera: Balige Publishing, 2024.

Vivian Siahaan and Rismon Hasiholan Sianipar. FEATURES-BASED MOTION ESTIMATION AND OBJECT TRACKING WITH PYTHON AND TKINTER. North Sumatera: Balige Publishing, 2024.

www.ingramcontent.com/pod-product-compliance
Lightning Source LLC
Chambersburg PA
CBHW062105220526
45471CB00010B/3605